SANDSTONE PUBL

THE UNBEATABLE AI

Glen Pattison is the director of Peak Performance International Pty Ltd. He is a Master Practitioner in NLP (Neuro Linguistic Programming), Time Line Therapy™ and Hypnosis, and is also a Personal Fitness Trainer.

Glen has extensive experience in the music industry. He has played drums for twenty-six years, and started teaching alongside some of the best musicians in the country when he was sixteen years old. During his career Glen has been involved in producing four albums, a number of hit singles and various television jingles and theme tracks. Drumming has also taken Glen throughout Australia, Europe and America, and has landed him numerous television and radio appearances. Combining his qualifications with his love of drumming, Glen has developed *The Unbeatable Advantage*—a three-step coaching system that has been designed to show you how to perform at your peak in your personal, sporting and business life.

Glen uses a number of drumming metaphors to convey a powerful but simple message—'It is about recognising that you have the power to take charge of your life, and by doing so, directing and focusing your efforts to reach new levels of success.'

The Unbeatable Advantage

The coaching system
for success in your personal,
business and sporting life

Glen Pattison

SANDSTONE BOOKS

For further information on product sales, seminars and consultations, contact:

Peak Performance International Pty Ltd
PO Box 529, Narrabeen NSW 2101, Australia.
Phone/fax +61 2 9981 6333, mobile 0412 499 101 or 0413 597 093.

Published in Australia 1999 by
Sandstone Publishing
Unit 3, 56 John Street
Leichhardt NSW 2040.
Phone +61 2 9552 3815, fax +61 2 9552 1538.

Production by
Neologica Print & Promotions
Surry Hills, NSW.
neologica@email.com.

National Library of Australia Cataloguing-in-Publication data:

Pattison, Glen.
The unbeatable advantage: the coaching system for
success in your personal, business and sporting life.

ISBN 1 86505 134 9

1. Self-actualization (Psychology). 2. Neurolinguistic programming.
3. Success. 4. Achievement motivation. 5. Performance. I. Title.

650.1

Printed in Australia by Griffin Press.

Contents

Preface

There is a saying that I try to live every day by and it is this—'Life is not a dress rehearsal'. I'm sure you have heard this said before, but the real power comes from acknowledging the message that is contained in these simple words. If you have, then you will understand that you have one chance at getting it right.

If we all get one chance at life, why are we so willing to hand the responsibility for our ultimate success and happiness over to someone else? Why are we so quick to find excuses for why we haven't achieved or succeeded?

I find it interesting that many people spend a great deal of time planning for something like their next vacation, but invest little or no time planning their life. Is your next vacation really more important than your long-term health, your career and your personal relationships? Success to me is about accepting responsibility. It is about recognising that you are in control of both the joys and failures you have experienced to date. It also means that you control the future direction of your life.

It's so simple to get stuck in the mind set of 'if only'—if only I had more money, if only I had a better education, if only I was ten kilos lighter, if only … if only … A healthier approach is to recognise that you have the power to change your life. If you are not happy with what life has given you, then realise that taking responsibility is the key to controlling your destiny. This book is here to help you take control of your life, to show you how to accept the ultimate responsibility for your success and happiness. This is very much a practical guide: your input and commitment are crucial. To take control of your destiny you must be responsible for your thoughts and actions; you must have real knowledge of what you are capable of and the skills required to lead you to success.

What is the fundamental principle behind *The Unbeatable Advantage*? It is about helping you improve your life.

In developing *The Unbeatable Advantage*, I realised that there was a real need for information that was affordable, accessible and easy to use. And in effect, it seems that what we are all searching for is a mentor or a wise friend—someone who has the time available to approach our problems objectively and practically to guide us to the right decision. Think of this book as a guide or workbook, close at hand, that you can refer to. The system outlined here will give you direction and focus, and therefore immediate results. And because drumming is what I know best, it seems only natural to base the system around the principals of drumming.

As a child I worked at the local golf driving range after school each day collecting golf balls. In return for two hours work I received fifty cents and a chocolate bar. I was fortunate enough as a child to see the sense in saving my money, so it came as no surprise to my parents that my first major purchase at the age of eight was a drum set.

I'd seen the set advertised in the newspaper for $100. Now, when you are earning fifty cents an afternoon, that's a lot of time spent picking up golf balls. Nevertheless, I'd decided that I had to have the drum set, so my family and I headed over to the other side of the city to pick it up. When I first saw it I remembered thinking that the drum set was seventeen years old—that made it nine years older than I was. In fact, the set was so old that not even my drum teacher knew how it all went together. But it was a drum set, and it was mine.

I became so involved with my drumming over the years that I would practise for hours and hours each day, even if it meant missing an afternoon at the beach with my friends. However, the practise paid off. At the age of sixteen my drumming ability was recognised by my music teacher. She convinced the school principal that I should be allowed to skip some classes each week for the opportunity to learn with one of the best drummers in Australia at the time. This was a real thrill for me because I was his only student.

If you know anything about drumming, then you will understand just how important it is for the drummer to have the highest level of skill and control in leading the band. If there was ever an outstanding example of this, it was this drummer. He was simply amazing. In fact, his drumming ability was awesome. He was able to play a drum roll that sounded like rapid machine gun fire on an area of the drum the size of a twenty-cent piece. As far as I was concerned, this guy was King.

What was interesting however, was the different person my father saw in this same drummer. Although he recognised and respected his musical ability, he also saw a person whose life was a wreck. He had made it to the top as a drummer in his country and had played with some of the best Australian and international acts, yet on a basic level he had come unstuck. For curtains he was using bedsheets, he had problems with both alcohol and drugs, his marriage had ended in divorce, and he had lost the love and respect of his children. So this guy had excelled in one area of his life at the expense of everything else.

After my first lesson I was bursting with excitement. I was learning from one of the best drummers and I was determined to be just like him. I'm sure that this concerned my parents, because to excel in one area of your life and neglect all others is a recipe for disaster. Around this time they gave me a book by Napolean Hill and W. Clement Stone called *Success Through a Positive Mental Attitude*. I can't begin to tell you what a role this book has played in my life. In fact, I remember after reading it over one weekend that I had learnt more about life from that single book than I had from all my years at school. This set me on a course of self-education that has included Hypnotherapy, Time Line Therapy™, Neuro Linguistic Programming and Personal Fitness Training, and these, combined with many late nights reading and research, have resulted in *The Unbeatable Advantage*.

Some of the issues that are addressed throughout the book and through my seminars and consultations include:

* increasing motivation

* developing a positive mental attitude, dealing with the past, present and future

* learning how to re-focus to get a 'fresh' start after a disturbing situation

* developing techniques to break self-limiting beliefs

* increasing self-confidence and self-esteem

* using physiology to take on the persona of a winner.

Working on these issues with the staff and management of some of this country's leading corporations and a number of elite athletes across all sporting disciplines, I have learned an important thing: that the human being is a remarkable creature, capable of anything he or she commits to doing.

If you take one gem of information from this book that helps you to achieve a more balanced and successful life, and you realise that you have the ability to be more than you think you can be, then I can say with confidence that the late nights, the early mornings, and indeed the effort involved in writing *The Unbeatable Advantage*, have all been justified.

Please enjoy.

— Glen Pattison, June 1999.

Acknowledgements

The biggest thank you must go to Felicity Kerr, my partner in business and in life. Without her this book would never have been written. Her commitment to this project was second to none. Thank you Felicity for your love, encouragement and dedication over the past three years.

To my parents, Rosemary and Allan Pattison. You have both been instrumental in me becoming the person I am today. The advice and learnings I took from the family chats around the dinner table have proven invaluable. Thank you also for your endless patience and understanding, without which my passion for drumming, and therefore this book, would never have been realised. I love you both. I would also like to thank Felicity's family for their ongoing interest and support while writing this book.

And thank you to my agent, Selwa Anthony. Selwa recognised the potential of this book from our first meeting. Since then she has continued to provide the advice and support that has resulted in the publication of this book, not to mention a flourishing speaking career. Thank you Selwa.

To two wonderful people at Sandstone Publishing, Ernie Mason and Graeme Clifford. Thank you both for believing not only in this book, but also in Felicity and me, and for having the tenacity to back a first time author. Your enthusiasm and hands on approach throughout the publication was fantastic.

And to Belinda Castles, our editor. Your feedback and advice have made all the difference—your suggestions really brought the book to life. Thank you also Belinda for your tireless patience and understanding. You were a real pleasure to work with.

And to Frank Corniola. Thank you for your faith in *The Unbeatable Advantage* from the outset. Your support and connections in the drumming community, both in Australia and overseas, have been extremely valuable. You are a man of your word, a true gentleman. Thank you Frank.

I would also like to thank all of our friends for their understanding and support while we were writing this book. Thanks for hanging in there. One friend in particular who has been great is Helen Hawkes. Thank you Helen, both for your friendship and your absolute professionalism—you have really helped fast-track the success of this book. A special thank you must also go to Mark Lewis. He was my original sounding board, and it was his encouragement and drive in the beginning that motivated me to put my thoughts down on paper.

And thank you to all of my clients, both in business and in sport. You have been wonderful to work with. Thank you for your support and commitment, and your belief in me and the concepts in this book.

Introduction

With the pace of things today, it is becoming increasingly difficult to achieve a balanced approach to life. Work is becoming more demanding, family life is increasingly challenging, money doesn't always stretch as far as one would like, and developing a solid relationship with a partner can sometimes be difficult. With all these demands placed upon us, we find ourselves spending much of our time and energy focusing on one or two areas of our lives, neglecting areas that are equally important.

We all know people who have excelled in a certain area of life at the expense of others. Take a quick look around and I'm sure you'll find a friend or co-worker whose ability at managing their finances is nothing short of outstanding. In fact, there probably isn't anything they can't afford, nowhere they haven't been and money just keeps finding its way to them. The sad thing is that this financial wealth often comes at the expense of poor health, miserable relationships and real problems with managing stress. The time and effort put into achieving financial success takes priority over fostering relationships with a partner, friends and family. It also means that very little time, if any, is spent looking after themselves—exercise tends to come last on their list, and good nutrition is often sacrificed for convenience. And it's not only financially successful people who have difficulties in balancing their lives.

As you can imagine, anyone who is at all serious about being a professional athlete must have an amazing level of health and fitness, and the long hours required to develop to such a level are gruelling. On any given day, professional athletes can spend between four and six hours training, and this is often in addition to working a full-time job. When you add up all these hours you can see that there is a real shortage of time available to do the everyday things that you and I take for granted. So in what areas of life would you expect a professional athlete to excel? Obviously in their health and fitness, and also in their goal setting. They recognise that they want real success from their sport and do everything they can to achieve that success. However, problems can begin to surface within their relationships because they have no time to give them. Financial management is also a real concern—most of their money is poured into buying the latest equipment and travelling to events. Time management can also be an issue—after devoting so much time to training there is very little left over for the other areas of life.

So what is the relevance of these examples? Simply to illustrate that being outstanding in one or two areas of life, at the expense of everything else, is not a real measure of success or happiness. Ask yourself this question: what is true success and happiness really about? I would suggest that the answer lies in achieving a balanced and finely-tuned life, and that is the message of this book.

The system emphasises the importance of achieving balance across eight major areas of life: Health and Fitness, Financial Management, Relationships, Leadership, Goal Setting, Communication, Time Management and Stress Management. Each of these topics is covered in a separate chapter. You can spend as much or as little time on each chapter as you feel is necessary.

The information contained in *The Unbeatable Advantage* can be applied to all facets of your personal, business, or sporting life. It is an informative, entertaining and educational approach to life that gives you access to cutting edge information and techniques that will help you reach new levels of happiness and success.

How to use this system

Step One—Scale Your Life©

Before you can achieve balance and success, you need to know exactly where in your life there is room for improvement. This can sometimes be difficult to be objective about, so I've created a method called 'Scale Your Life' to help you identify your individual strengths and problem areas. It involves rating yourself on a scale of one to ten in the eight areas of life.

To Scale Your Life, consider the questions starting on page 4.

Step Two—Fine-tune Your Life©

With many of the people I work with, it becomes clear that something has been holding them back from performing at their peak. This step will help you find out what is holding you back and how to overcome the obstacle, using a simple key called 'The A.S.K. Key©'—it represents attitude, skill and knowledge. Once you have identified an area of your life that you would like to improve, simply A.S.K. yourself if it is your attitude, skill or knowledge (or a combination of the three) that is holding you back from excelling.

If you'd like to know more about Attitude, have a read through the section in Step Two (page 9). It looks at how to create a winning attitude by controlling your beliefs, your focus and your physiology. It will also show you how to eliminate your self-limiting beliefs—the limitations you place on yourself that are rarely true, yet hold you back from achieving your full potential. How often have you let a belief about yourself stop you from doing something new or exciting because you thought you might mess it up?

There is also a section that relates directly to the concept of Knowledge. This was put together to give you an advantage when it comes to accessing and recalling information. You'll learn the secrets to developing a great memory; how to increase your ability to learn; and how to increase both your reading speed and effectiveness. These tools are beneficial when it comes to acquiring the knowledge needed to improve a specific area of life.

Step Three—Set Your Groove©

There are four simple steps involved in Setting Your Groove, but together they take less than one minute.

This technique shows you how to develop a positive mental focus that will enable you to turn a negative state into a positive state. It can also be used as a relaxation technique that clears your mind, giving you a fresh platform to work from. It is great for moving beyond an upsetting phone call in the morning that would otherwise throw you off course for the entire day, or that one terrible shot on the first green that would otherwise set you up for another seventeen lousy holes of golf. Having said this, how you use the system, and the information contained in *The Unbeatable Advantage*, is a personal decision. You may prefer to read the book from front to back, or for more immediate results simply follow the system—Scale Your Life, choose an area you'd like to set about improving, apply The A.S.K. Key theory, and to stay on track, become familiar with Set Your Groove.

Monitor your progress

It can seem like a slow road to success unless you are able to look back and see how far you've come. You can monitor your progress over the next twelve months—twelve smaller drum skins are included at the back of the book so you can congratulate yourself on your improvements or see exactly where you still have some work to do.

This book is about developing the attitude, skills and knowledge necessary to manage your own life successfully, so decide for yourself the most effective approach to improving and monitoring your life, and above all enjoy the process of taking control of your future successes!

Step One—Scale Your Life

So what's all this got to do with drumming? To understand how it all fits together we need to take a look at how a drum actually works.

The view in Figure 1 is taken looking down onto a drum. You can see that there are eight lugs around the side of the drum, and each lug is responsible for applying tension to a particular part of the drum skin from the rim directly into the centre. To get the best sound from the drum, all of the eight lugs must be balanced and finely tuned. For an optimum sound it is not enough for two, three or even four lugs to be tuned—the tension must be evenly balanced across the entire skin.

The drum and how it applies to life

The drum is a perfect metaphor for life—like the drum, life also has eight major areas (see Figure 2).

How much better would your life be without disappointing personal relationships, problems managing your finances, or

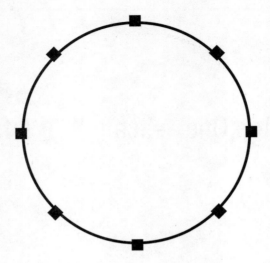

Figure 1: The eight tuning lugs on a drum

stress about things that haven't happened (and probably won't)? Each area needs attention for balance and success.

Scaling of the drum

Looking at Figure 3, you can see that the scaling works from the rim of the drum to the centre—the rim represents zero and the centre of the drum represents ten.

When drumming, playing consistently in the six to ten area (the centre region) is quite difficult, and requires skill and practise. The effort required to play in this area of the drum is much greater than in the zero to five region—each step towards ten requires the drummer to be more disciplined and to apply a greater deal of concentration and effort. To play on this part of the skin, the drummer really has to perform. Of the entire skin, it is the centre that gives the best sound.

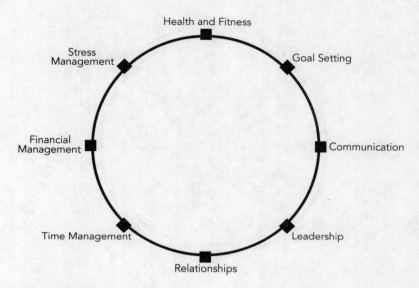

Figure 2: The eight areas of life

If you have the opportunity to watch a highly skilled drummer perform, you'll notice that they are able to play a drum roll on an area of the skin that is no larger than a twenty-cent-piece. On the other hand, inexperienced drummers are sloppier—they will occasionally hit the centre region, but more often than not their playing is in the outer region.

The same principle can be applied to life—the zero to five range in each of the eight areas is where many people are at. At this level, life doesn't seem to be too bad, but it's not great either—there is definitely room for improvement. If we return to the thought that 'Life is not a dress rehearsal', life lived at this level seems a terrible waste, doesn't it?

Moving towards the next level—the six-to-ten region—requires you to be more focused with each step you take. You need to be honest with yourself—question how your life is

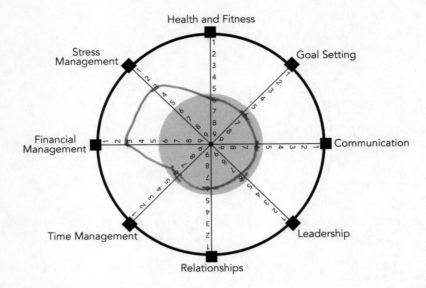

Figure 3: Scaling of the drum

now, and also how determined you are to improve the direction that your life is taking. Each step that you take towards ten requires a higher level of effort and determination. This region represents success in each of the areas.

To achieve your desired level of success, you must pay attention to the eight areas of life. Being tuned in one, two or even three areas will not give you any real level of satisfaction or achievement in life. Like a drum, you should be balanced and finely tuned in all eight areas for optimum performance. Consider your answers to these questions:

Health and Fitness

* Do you have enough energy to accomplish everything that you want to do throughout the day?

* At the end of the day, do you arrive home full of vitality or do you head straight for the couch?

* Do you know what foods help your body function at its peak, or which foods drain you of energy?

Goal Setting

* Do you find that the things you wanted to achieve when you were younger are forgotten about or abandoned now?

* Where do you want to be in one, five or twenty years from now?

* Do you have your goals written down?

* How often do you review your goals?

Communication

* How easy do you find it to develop rapport with people?

* Do you find it simple or difficult to get your point across in a conversation?

* Do you enjoy social events or do they make you feel insecure?

Leadership

* What skills do you have that other people admire?

* Do you have the ability to influence others in a positive way?

* In a group situation, do you prefer to take the lead or to sit back and follow?

Relationships

* Do you sometimes feel that your relationship is in a rut, or that your partner tends to be low on your list of priorities?

* How rewarding is your current relationship, both for yourself and your partner?

* When was the last time you did something special for your partner, other than on Valentine's Day?

Time Management

* How much time do you have to do the things you really want to do, not that your partner or children or work command of you?

* Do you leave the things that you want to accomplish till last? What priority do you put on your personal goals?

* How do you approach the things that you need to accomplish each day?

Financial Management

* Do you prefer to save for something special or are you more inclined to spend your money as you earn it?

* Are you always short of money by payday, or do you plan and budget your expenses?

* Have you ever taken the time to set and follow a budget?

* If you continue to manage your finances as you do today, what level of wealth can you expect to enjoy in the future?

Stress Management

* How often do you find yourself worrying about things that have already happened and you can do nothing about?

* How much time do you spend stressing over things that never eventuate?

* Do you often eat quickly because you feel rushed?

* Do you worry about work, even when you are not there?

Now that you understand the scaling of the drum and have taken some time to honestly answer the questions for each area, it's possible to Scale Your Life.

Some people will find this step exciting, while for others the exercise may be a little unsettling, but please persist—this is the first step in taking control of your life to ensure future success. It's simple to live each day without honestly addressing the direction your life is taking. You can pretend that your life is shaping up just fine, but taking control and achieving success and happiness is about congratulating yourself on your strengths and also identifying and working on the areas that you'd like to improve.

Now it's your turn ...

Using Figure 4, look at the eight areas of your life and plot on a scale of one to ten (one being least desirable and ten being ideal) where you are at this point in time. You might like to refer back to the questions on the previous pages.

Once you have scaled your life, it's simply a matter of joining each of the points. This step enables you to identify your strengths and weaknesses. Joining the points on each 'spoke' allows you to see the balance and tuning of your own drum, life. This gives your life real meaning by highlighting your strong and weak spots. You can see exactly where your life is unbalanced. It really shows you where you are at: try it on the diagram to see the direction your life is taking.

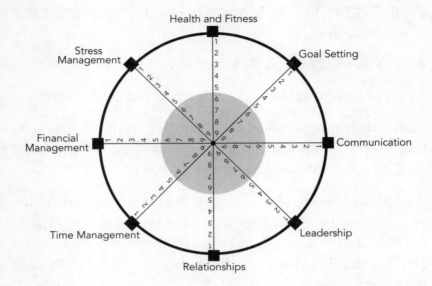

Figure 4: Scale Your Life

Step Two—Fine-tune Your Life

It's not enough simply to acknowledge that there are certain areas in your life that you'd like to improve—the real power comes from deciding to make some real and lasting changes that will bring about the results you want. So what I'd like to do here is to think about the reasons why you should look at addressing the areas in your life in need of development.

Take some time now to consider how you feel about the results from Scale Your Life. Do you want your future to be similar to your past? Because one thing is certain in life—if you keep doing more of the same then you will get more of the same. In other words, if you want your life to take on new meaning and to experience new successes, then you must be prepared to make some significant changes to the way you do things.

Ask yourself this question—why settle for a relationship, health or finances that are anything less than outstanding, when you can achieve a level of success beyond the one you have now? What has accepting a life that is less than outstanding cost you so far? Consider the emotional cost, the financial cost and the physical cost—and what it will cost you if you continue to live tomorrow as you do today.

If you continue doing the same things that you are doing now, how will your life be in one, five, or even twenty years from now? Will you still have the same job? Or problems managing money? Where can you see your life heading? What level of success can you see for yourself?

In answering these questions, you first need to decide what success means to you. Of course, success is a very personal concept, and there is no right or wrong answer. Success means different things to different people, but let me suggest that it is something that involves every area of life—your health, your relationships, your finances—and excelling in one area at the cost of another is not a balanced or healthy approach to life.

So how do you Fine-tune Your Life for success? Well, read on …

How to Fine-tune Your Life

As background to the second step in the system let's look at how a drum is tuned.

The key used to tune the lugs on a drum is called a drum key. To get a great sound from the drum, each of the lugs is worked on turn by turn, applying tension directly into the centre, until the tension across the drum skin is just right. Take a look at Figure 5.

Now unfortunately, life doesn't come with a tuning key. But what I'd like to share with you is a tool that I've developed that will allow you to achieve balance and fine-tuning by working

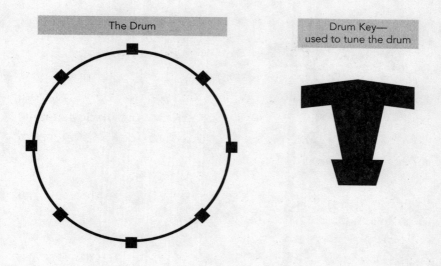

Figure 5: Balance and fine-tuning

on each area of your life—it's called the A.S.K. Key. It represents Attitude, Skill and Knowledge.

The A.S.K. Key is a simple yet highly effective tool that will enable you to fine-tune those areas of your life that are causing you problems or pain. It will help you improve your current situation so that you can expect more from life in every single aspect of it (see Figure 6).

Attitude is determined by your beliefs (experiences and references) and your state (focus and physiology). I'll explain a little more fully what I mean by 'beliefs' and 'state' later in this chapter.

Skill is your ability to do something well.

Knowledge is knowing the appropriate information to complete the task at hand.

The key to fine-tune your life

A = Attitute

S = Skill

K = Knowledge

Figure 6: The A.S.K. Key

Let's test The A.S.K. Key theory

To show you just how powerful The A.S.K. Key can be, consider an Olympic gold medallist. Do you think if their attitude, skill or knowledge was anything less than brilliant, they would even be in contention for such a prestigious and honourable medal? Would they be in a position to receive worldwide recognition and respect for their efforts?

Another situation that highlights the power behind The A.S.K. Key is that of a sports person who was about to be given a once in a lifetime opportunity to represent his country. This individual had worked really hard over the years to get to where he was. He had put in more practise each session than his teammates and did all he could to ensure that his level of skill at his sport was outstanding. Because he loved his sport so much, he also devoted a great deal of time and energy into researching all he could on it. He knew all the latest and proven theories and made a point of spending time with the best players in the game to ensure that his knowledge too was outstanding. However, he had a problem with his attitude.

Because of his success in the game he had become arrogant. He thought that he was above not only the rules of the game, but that he could also do and say what he wanted when he was away from the game. This was where he fell down. He had a general disregard for other people, and this disregard was noticed by the people who mattered. Because of his poor attitude, he missed out on what may well have proven to be his only opportunity to represent his country on an international basis.

If you are considering applying for a job promotion, you will find this story interesting. An employee had been working for the same company for close to seven years. He'd had his share of small promotions in the past, but this time the promotion he was interested in was for a more senior position in the company. He was by no means an outstanding employee. In fact, he did just enough to meet his job requirements and to keep his position. However, he felt that because he had worked for the company for seven years, he was entitled to the promotion. After all, his seven years' experience meant that his level of knowledge and skill were relatively up to speed, but it was his attitude that was holding him back from succeeding. Needless to say, he missed out on the promotion, because senior management felt that it was in their best interest not to have someone with a bad attitude leading other employees.

To test the power of The A.S.K. Key theory and how it applies to your life, start by looking at the areas in which you scored highest (your strengths). Ask yourself if one or more of the three elements (attitude, skill or knowledge) had been missing whether you could have achieved the same level of success. Also, if you were to improve these areas, which element would you still need to work on? I'm sure you'll find that for any measure of achievement in your life, you too must have the right combination of attitude, skill and knowledge.

Now take a look at the areas that you scored lowest in and ask yourself if it is inadequate attitude, skill, or knowledge that is limiting your success. It may not be obvious straight away, but if you are honest with yourself, you'll soon realise which element (or combination of elements) you need to work on to achieve what you want in life.

If you know your attitude needs work then read onto the next section, in which 'beliefs' and 'state' are explained. It shows you how to develop a winning attitude—an attitude that propels you onwards in achieving your goals. With a winning attitude, you control your focus, your beliefs and your physiology; therefore you are in control of the level of success in your life. A winning attitude is about recognising that you are responsible for the direction of your life, rather than dishing out blame and looking for excuses for why you haven't succeeded.

If your level of skill is holding you back then let me suggest that practise is the mother of skill, and that your level of skill is determined by the amount of time you spend putting your knowledge into practise. For example, my goal with drumming was to become a top-class drummer. To do this, I recognised that having the right attitude, combined with a high level of knowledge would not see me achieve my goal if I didn't follow through with at least six hours of practise each day to develop my skill. Improving your level of skill may simply require that you put into action what you already know, or you might need to start by gaining the right information. You can do this by reading the chapter of this book that relates to the area of life that you would like to improve, and then put that information to work.

It may be that your level of knowledge is not as developed as it needs to be. If this is the case then go directly to the relevant chapter on that area, and look at the section on Knowledge itself—there are some great tips on how best to access and recall information that will help bring your level of knowledge up to speed.

Attitude

Your attitude is a combination of:

* your beliefs (your references or experiences)

* your state (your focus and physiology)

Achieving what you want from life will be much easier if you have a winning attitude. So let's take a closer look at what makes a winning attitude.

Beliefs—the first step in developing a winning attitude

I'd like to start by having you ask yourself which statement is true: 'life is fantastic' or 'life is lousy'. If your life is full of love and happiness and you're surrounded by positive, supportive people, you'll probably believe that life is fantastic. On the other hand, if your life has been really tough, if your childhood was sad, or you've been out of work for a while, then you may believe that your life is lousy. Your answer will of course depend on your beliefs, and your beliefs depend on the experiences you've had and your references in life. There is no right or wrong answer—it depends on whatever you decide is true for you.

Have you ever thought about how important your beliefs are in shaping your personality and how you see the world, and in turn how others perceive you? You see, your beliefs will determine how you act in certain situations, how you think towards certain people and what decisions you make in life.

What is a belief?

A belief is something that you feel certain about—it is something that you have come to accept as true. However, you were not born with a predetermined set of beliefs. In fact, all beliefs start out as ideas, and as we go through life we have many experiences, some that support our ideas and others that don't. Now, the more support your ideas receive, the stronger your beliefs become.

Your beliefs have the power to control your life, simply because when you believe something, it controls what you focus on and what you feel. Your beliefs are also extremely powerful in terms of how you look at life, and especially how you look at yourself. They can be both positive and negative, empowering or disempowering, and of course they don't have to be true. In fact, you can develop a belief about anything as long as you have enough references to back it up. It's important then, that you choose beliefs that are supportive and positive.

The power of beliefs

Your beliefs are self-fulfilling. They are so powerful that whatever you truly believe will eventuate. Henry Ford understood this when he said 'If you believe that you can or you can't, then you're right'.

Your beliefs can be so powerful that they can bring you either success or failure. The most disempowering beliefs are our self-limiting beliefs—beliefs that we have about ourselves that hold us back in some way. We are too quick to accept self-limiting beliefs, ignoring any references that they may in fact be false. Why? Because we've decided that they are true based on negative information we've taken in.

One example of how self-limiting beliefs can stop you from achieving your full potential is that of a top-performing sales-man. My client had worked selling medium-priced family vehicles up to $50,000. He felt comfortable with the people he was selling to, and in fact he felt in control of the situation—he was able to relate to his customers, he was confident and his product knowledge was excellent. He was outstanding at what he did, so much so that he was headhunted by one of the luxury vehicle dealers. But this is where he came unstuck. When he was suddenly forced to deal with a more demanding and older clientele prepared to spend much more on a vehicle, he believed that he wasn't up to the job. Believing that he wasn't 'good enough' to sell a vehicle worth $150,000, his sales dropped dramatically. So first we set about determining why he held the belief. From here we worked on eliminating it and replacing his old belief with a new, empowering and posi-tive belief about what he was capable of. When you start to question your self-limiting beliefs, they immediately become less powerful and have less of a hold on you. Asking the right questions will eventually dissolve their power.

It's important to realise that the limitations you place on your-self are rarely true—they exist in your mind only. Simply deciding to change your limiting beliefs can change the direc-tion of your life in a dramatic way. Do you really want a life full of happiness, love, success and prosperity? It's your choice. You have the ability to change your life, but you have to be willing to make the effort involved.

You can choose to believe anything about yourself, either positive or negative, and what you decide to believe will determine the life that you lead. It's important that you recognise what limiting beliefs you have about yourself and work to change them. Think in terms of how you want to be, or how you'd like a certain situation to be—move towards what you want in life. If you change your beliefs then you can expect a change in your attitude, your behaviour, and in what you can expect to receive from life.

We've all seen the people who have achieved amazing things—simply because they believed they could—and followed their belief through with absolute conviction. And you can bet that in most cases their success didn't come easily either—more often than not these people had to overcome huge obstacles.

Did you realise that Beethoven and Thomas Edison were deaf, Julius Caesar suffered from epilepsy, Charles Dickens was lame, and Andrew Carnegie started working for just four dollars a month? These men didn't let their disabilities, lack of education or humble beginnings limit their success. Simply by channelling the immense power of their minds, they achieved absolutely everything they set out to do.

You have the ability to achieve what you want in life. When you remove your self-limiting beliefs you'll find that life will be willing to give you all that you ask of it, as long as it doesn't harm anyone else. Imagine for just a minute what your life could be like if you used the immense power of your mind to create empowering beliefs—the kind that would give you the life you wanted. Well, the first step is to eliminate the beliefs that have been holding you back from achieving your full potential.

How to eliminate your self-limiting beliefs

Your beliefs are extremely powerful. They command how you think, how you feel and how you act. They are so deeply engraved that we don't even question their commands. We don't question whether or not our beliefs are true, yet we allow our beliefs to determine what is possible and what is not. If you want to make any real and substantial change in your life, you need to change how you think about yourself. The next four steps will allow you to eliminate your disempowering beliefs.

What is the benefit?

People do things for one of two reasons—to avoid pain or for gain. Take the example of trying to motivate a mule. You could either tempt it with a carrot and motivate the mule by gain, or hit it with a stick and force it to do what you want by inflicting a certain amount of pain. So when deciding if you should eliminate a self-limiting belief, ask yourself if you will benefit by changing your belief, that is will you avoid pain or move towards gain? If you won't benefit by changing your belief then don't—you have to really want and need to change your existing belief system. There has to be enough gain associated with changing or enough pain if you don't.

Scramble your existing belief

Picture in your mind the situation that is bothering you: Run the situation through your mind as a movie. Watch everything that happens without any judgement. Don't allow yourself to attach any emotion to the events you see.

Picture it as a cartoon: Now picture the same scene, but this time turn it into a cartoon. Make the scene hilarious. Play some silly music in your head. Try running it backward at high speed, and then run it even faster, this time forward. Change the colour and brightness, and if someone (including yourself) said something to create the limiting belief, then turn that person into a humorous cartoon character with a comical voice. You can make whatever adjustments you like until the whole scene loses all its significance. Make sure you have some fun doing this. Run it through differently, both forwards and backwards, ten or so times.

Think about the situation that was bothering you: How do you feel now? You should feel completely different. In fact, it might be difficult for you to even recall how you were feeling originally. The situation should no longer be limiting in any way.

This might seem like a simple way to change something that has been holding you back for so long, and it is, but it does work. Your mind thinks in pictures, and if you can change the pictures in your mind, then you can effectively change how you feel toward a situation. The more you practise the technique, the better you'll become, and the results will happen much faster each time.

Visualisation

After getting rid of your old belief you need to replace it with a new, empowering belief. Picture yourself as you'd like to be—it may be in a fantastic, loving relationship, or sitting behind your new desk after successfully achieving the promotion you were after. What would you be wearing? What kind of people would you surround yourself with? How would you feel? What would you be saying? Picture your ideal scene in as much detail as possible. Use all of your senses—your sight, smell, taste, touch and hearing.

Modelling

Modelling is a short cut to success. It involves using people who have been successful in ways you admire as role models. Make an effort to look for and study people who have made lasting changes, and who have secured the results you're after.

Modelling is extremely effective when it comes to learning and replacing old behaviour patterns with new ones. In fact, your beliefs, attitudes, behaviour patterns and values were developed when you were growing up, by modelling your friends and family, so the technique is not new. This is different though, because you are making an active choice about which role models you use. If you are going to make the most of your new beliefs, then why not speed up the process by modelling someone who has already achieved success. It's a great way of making a new belief part of how you operate today.

State—the second step in developing a winning attitude

Wouldn't it be great to be able to put yourself in a positive, powerful frame of mind whenever you wanted to? Take a moment to imagine how much more you could achieve from life by simply being able to control how you felt in any situation. A great deal of the secret is to understand the importance of 'state'. Let me explain.

Imagine that you are a salesperson. Now picture a customer approaching you for help. It has been a long day, and not a terribly good one at that. You can think of a dozen other places you'd rather be, and you are not particularly keen to offer your help—after all, you're due to go home in ten minutes. Now put yourself in the position of the customer. Can you imagine what you would look like as you approach the customer? You would probably be moving slowly, with an uninterested look on your face, and your focus would be more on leaving for home than on satisfying your customer. What kind of impression of you do think your customer would have, based on your actions? I'm sure you wouldn't close the sale.

Now imagine the impact if you were able to turn this negative situation into one that was powerful and purposeful—if you were able to put yourself into a positive, powerful frame of mind whenever you wanted to. You would be perceived as keen, attentive, and alert rather than bored and uninterested. You would be judged as someone who is a pleasure to deal with, who is attentive and willing to go out of their way to ensure that their customers' needs are met. Do you think that this impression would help close the deal? Most definitely. You'll find that either way, be it a positive or negative state, people are quick to label you. 'Wasn't he a great guy to deal with', or 'He was one of the worst people I have ever bought from—I won't be buying anything here again'.

These examples show that how you feel at any given moment is determined by two things—what you focus on and how you move your body (your physiology), and these combined are known as 'state'. Most of the time, the way you react to a situation is automatic—you are not conscious of how or why you respond the way you do. So your state can be either empowering or disempowering, and can work either for or against you. It is an extremely powerful tool in changing how you're feeling about someone or something. So let's take a look at the importance of physiology.

Physiology

Have you ever thought about the connection between how you feel emotionally and how you feel physically? To show you just how strong the connection is I want you to focus on feeling fantastic, but I'd like you to stand with your head down, your shoulders slouched, with a long face. Are you feeling great yet? It's impossible, isn't it, because the way you move your body is extremely powerful in influencing how you feel. Trying to feel terrible is just as impossible when you stand with your shoulders back, your head up high, your chest out and a huge grin across your face.

So you can see that how you move changes the way you behave, the way you feel and how you think about almost any situation. It's important to understand that your emotions affect your body and in turn your physiology also affects how you feel.

Take a minute to think about someone successful and happy. How do they walk and talk? What are their facial expressions like? What gestures do they use? What is the tone of their voice like? You'll find that their thoughts and their body movements compliment each other—they are positive and empowering.

Ask yourself what your physiology says about you. What impression do you think you are giving of your state at this moment? If you're not getting the results you want in life, chances are you're not conditioning your body to receive success. To achieve your potential, it's important to learn how to tap your positive, powerful states. To do this, think back to a situation when you felt fantastic. Remember in as much detail as possible your breathing, your facial expressions, your posture, your gestures. What were you thinking? What were you saying? Recall everything you can about that time. Make it come to life. Feel it! See it! Hear it!

Understand that you can reproduce this state any time you need to feel empowered, simply by thinking and acting as you did then. Being able to access a peak state is essential for you to achieve your goals. You see, being able to put yourself in a peak state that supports your goals will go a long way in determining whether or not you succeed in life. Almost any situation can be made to work for you simply by accessing positive physiology.

Now let's look at focus—the other essential ingredient for developing an empowering state.

Focus

How easy do you think it is to change how you're feeling now? Do you think you could do so without too much effort? Before you answer this question, try this exercise. I want you to focus on feeling great, just for a minute or so. Think about something that happened in the past that made you feel fantastic. If you think about it, picture it and focus on it long enough, in no time at all you'll be feeling as if you were in the situation once again. Do you think you could manage to feel lousy with just as little effort? Of course you could, and a big part of the answer to my question depends on your focus.

Your focus controls how you view the world and how you experience the things that happen to you. Your focus will also determine how you feel and how you behave. All too often we focus on the negative, yet the choice of what we can notice in any situation is almost unlimited. It's important to realise that you alone have the power to control your focus. Changing your focus is one of the most important ways of changing how you feel about absolutely anything. Remember, it's just as easy to put yourself in a positive, powerful state as it is to feel down and sorry for yourself.

If you want to improve any area of your life you have to become aware of what you focus on. The next time you feel tempted to complain about a colleague or relative, think about whether the situation is really that bad, or whether you are complaining out of habit. If you continue to focus on the negative side of each situation, then life will continue to serve you with more negative situations to focus on. However, change your focus, make it powerful, and you'll find yourself heading in the direction you want your life to take—focus on what you want from life and where you want to go, rather than dwelling on what life hasn't given you.

The power of questions in deciding your focus

Asking empowering questions will give you empowering answers.

We ask ourselves hundreds of questions each day. In fact, most of our day is taken up by asking questions and finding the answers, and it is these questions and answers that determine our focus. If you want to change the direction of your life then you need to change the questions you ask, both of yourself and others. Questions are extremely powerful—they determine your focus, they determine how you feel and how you think.

Have you ever noticed that the successful people around you are the people asking quality questions? They direct their focus by controlling the questions they ask. Asking quality questions directs your focus and forces your mind to come up with the quality answers you're looking for. Quite simply, asking empowering questions will give you empowering answers.

Many people ask lousy questions yet expect great answers— great answers only come from asking outstanding questions. What are some of the questions you ask yourself on a regular basis? Are they positive and uplifting, or negative and demotivating? You'll probably find that most of the questions you ask are disempowering, simply because it's what you've been taught. For example, 'Why can't I lose weight?' 'Why am I always broke?' 'Why does this always happen to me?' 'Why doesn't it ever work out for me?' 'Why did he/she do this to me?' The list goes on and on, but I'm sure you get the picture. Questions like this force your mind to concentrate on the negative aspect of a situation.

Stop asking the wrong questions and start asking those that will give you purposeful answers. You can't expect your life to be fantastic if the questions you're asking are anything less than outstanding. Make your questions work for you. Focus on finding the solution, and not on the problem itself. Turning the above questions around, you might ask, 'How can I reach my ideal weight?' 'How can I achieve greater personal wealth?' 'How can I make sure that next time I'll be in control of what happens to me?' Some of the most important questions we can ask ourselves when times are tough are, 'What have I learned from this? Would I behave differently if the same thing happened again?'

Each set of questions will determine your focus, and therefore your results. The situation doesn't change—the resources are given, yet the outcome depends greatly upon the questions you ask, which in turn will determine your focus. Train your mind to ask empowering questions. Ask yourself these empowering questions over and over again and expect answers that are powerful and purposeful. Asking questions that give powerful answers will have a direct impact on the direction of your life.

You can see that your attitude can help you achieve amazing results in life. Having a winning attitude allows you to perform at your peak, and this is so important in developing success throughout your life. However, having the right attitude alone is not enough—your level of knowledge and skill are also essential.

Skill

Skill is the ability you have to do something well. Most people have a combination of natural skills and those they have achieved through perseverance.

I know that you are familiar with the saying 'practise makes perfect', and that's the concept behind skill. Practise is the mother of skill. Succeeding in any area of life means developing the right attitude and knowing the right information and putting these into practise until you have mastered the situation.

Remember, success comes from having the right balance of each of the three concepts—attitude, skill, and knowledge

Knowledge

Having a winning attitude is extremely important, but without knowing the right information the level of success that you achieve will be limited. For example, how can you hope to improve your level of health and fitness without knowing what foods to eat or what exercises to do? Or how to achieve financial prosperity if you know very little about money management?

With the world moving faster today than ever before, there is an increased pressure to keep up, or better still, ahead of what is happening, and this means knowing how to make the most of the information available to you.

This section on 'Knowledge' has been put together to give you the advantage when it comes to accessing and recalling information. The areas covered are Learning, Memory and Reading.

Power Learning

The idea behind Power Learning is to show you how you can learn more quickly than you do now.

It seems that the human brain is a resource that is not being used efficiently or effectively. In fact, studies have shown that humans use only one to two per cent of their total brainpower—this is alarming when you consider that our mental capabilities are our greatest resource. This means that the vast majority—ninety-eight to ninety-nine per cent—of our brain is not being used; hard to believe isn't it? Try to imagine what you could achieve if you were able to access just another one to two per cent of your brainpower!

Although it may seem a little ambitious, Soviet and Bulgarian researchers claim that we have the ability to increase our learning by up to sixty times. Whatever the level of improvement, your brainpower is there waiting to be tapped, so let's get on with it.

To improve the way you learn and make it enjoyable, you first need to recognise just how capable you are of learning—the potential of your mind power is almost unlimited. It is also important to eliminate any negative feelings you have about learning. Power Learning isn't like the 'learning' you did in school. In fact, it couldn't be more different; Power Learning is about being relaxed and open to the information.

Relax your learning

Relaxing your entire body and mind will help remove any stress and anxiety, and is the first step in accessing your mind's potential. Relaxing not only helps you remember information, but also helps you recall it when it's needed. The more relaxed you can be, the more effective your learning will be.

Think back to a time when you tried to remember someone's name, but couldn't. No matter how hard you tried the name wouldn't come to you, but as soon as you relaxed the name appeared in your head! Relaxing isn't something that comes easily to everyone, so it may take a little practise. The following techniques should help you reach a relaxed state.

How to reach a relaxed state

Before you sit down to absorb any information, take five minutes in a quite place where you won't be disturbed and find a comfortable position. Close your eyes and focus on your breathing; follow each breath in and then out, making sure to take a deep, slow breath each time. Then concentrate on relaxing every part of your body, from your feet up to your head, and then back down again. Feel each part of your body unwind. Remember a time when you felt totally relaxed—maybe it was on your favourite vacation or lying in the park on a Sunday afternoon. Remember the total experience in as much detail as possible.

After five minutes you'll find your body is totally relaxed and your mind focused and alert. This is your peak state for improving your ability to learn.

Using music to help you learn

Listening to relaxing music while studying is another important step in increasing your ability to learn and recall the information when it's needed. I have found that one of the most effective types of music is that of the baroque composers of the seventeenth and eighteenth centuries.

Baroque music helps increase your ability to learn by putting you in a relaxed frame of mind. Like your heart, it works on sixty beats per minute, and your body and mind seem to naturally float along with the slow, soothing music. Some of the most popular baroque composers are Bach, Vivaldi, Telemann, Handel and Mozart. Playing the largo (slow) movements from concertos in the background while you're studying will lower your blood pressure, slow your pulse, and put you in a state of relaxed alertness—and that means more effective learning.

Making your own Power Learning tapes to use while learning is easy and effective. You'll be able to listen to your tape before going to bed, while washing the dishes, going for a walk, taking a bath or at any other time that suits you.

To start with, find twenty to thirty minutes of baroque music (any longer and your brain is unable to absorb the information into your long-term memory). Record your information by reading it out aloud while playing the baroque music in the background continuously. Record four seconds of information

(with the music in the background), then stop speaking for the next four seconds, then record another four seconds of information, and then stop speaking for the next four seconds. Repeat this again and again for the full twenty to thirty minutes of your tape. If this sounds a little complicated, try studying with the music playing softly as you work.

Colour your learning

Have you ever noticed how inquisitive children are? They're constantly asking questions, from the time they get up in the morning right through until their bedtime each night. It's no coincidence that a child's life is full of exploration. In fact, their ability to learn is at its peak in their early years. As adults we often stop exploring, we stop asking questions of ourselves and others. Consider how much more we could experience if we were to open our minds to think like a child—all you need to do is to train yourself to start asking questions again.

Asking questions is a fantastic way not only to expand your learning as an adult, but also to improve understanding, increase creativity and stimulate your imagination—areas we tend to close off over the years as we get older. We've gone from learning in an environment that is happy, bright, active and stimulating to one that is strict and unimaginative. Well, it's time to relax your thoughts and to let your creativity flow once again.

You'll find that your ability to learn will increase dramatically when your mind is visually stimulated. Forget that as an adult you are supposed you to be neat and tidy—neatness can in fact hinder your ability to learn. When you're studying or making notes for yourself, break all the rules—use as many different coloured pens and markers as possible; be creative; be messy;

exaggerate certain points; write in a different style or size; use pictures and shapes—anything you find fun and interesting. Remember, your mind learns best when it is visually stimulated.

Simply by making these techniques a part of your study routine, you'll be well on your way to accessing some of that brainpower that's waiting to be used!

Power Memory

Wouldn't it be great to be able to remember the grocery list without having to write it down, or the name of the person you were introduced to a minute ago, or the dental appointment you made for Monday, or was it Tuesday?

Before you can increase the power of your memory, it's a good idea to understand how your memory works. It may surprise you to know that your mind thinks totally in pictures, and not in words or in sounds, or in any other way. It may surprise you even more to know that your mind remembers virtually everything that you experience. I can hear you saying 'Yeah, sure—I can't remember what I had for breakfast today, let alone something I saw or thought about years ago'. The problem isn't your inability to remember the information; it's not knowing how to store the information properly in the first place.

How your memory is organised

Your memory works like a filing cabinet with three main drawers; how organised the drawers are depends upon the power and organisation of your memory. Basically, the three areas (or drawers) where you can store information are the short-term memory, the long-term accessible memory, and the long-term inaccessible memory.

* your short-term memory lets you remember things you experience anywhere from a few seconds to a few hours ago

* your long-term accessible memory includes all the information that is simply impossible for you to forget, like your own name and telephone number

* your long-term inaccessible memory contains all the information that doesn't fit into the other memory areas.

Many people have memories that look something like a teenager's bedroom floor; things are scattered all over the place, there's no particular spot for anything, and good luck if you're trying to find something important. If this sounds familiar then don't worry, because the following techniques will show you how to remember things much more easily.

Linking

This is a great technique for remembering a list of items, such as the groceries. The first step in remembering your list is to have a place to attach or link the information to. You then need to link in a crazy way something you know (something that's stored in your accessible long-term memory that's impossible for you to forget) with something that you want to remember. One of the easiest ways to do this is to make a body parts list, using parts of your body to link the information to. To make your body parts list you need to decide on ten areas of your body, starting from your head down and commit them to memory in a sequential order. For example, one might be your hair, two your mouth, three your shoulders, four your chest, five your stomach and so on. There's no right or wrong way to develop your body parts list, as long as the parts are in sequential order. Once you've remembered which body part goes with each number, the rest is easy.

Let's take a look at a grocery list: a dozen eggs, one loaf or bread, six bananas, one lettuce and a notepad. To remember these groceries, you need to link each item to a part of your body from your body parts list. So the dozen eggs will be linked with your hair (number one from the list above), the loaf of bread will be linked to your mouth, the lettuce to your shoulders, the six bananas to your chest, and the notepad to your stomach.

When you are linking the items to your body parts list, picture in your mind a clear, yet strange link between each item you want to remember and the body part it belongs to. Creating a vivid picture of the information you want to remember is the next step, and this is where the fun begins.

For example, picture the dozen eggs being squashed into your hair; feel the shells crack open. With the loaf of bread, you might picture yourself cramming freshly baked wholemeal bread into your mouth, piece by piece, until the entire loaf is squashed in tightly.

To develop the right kind of pictures, there are a few things to keep in mind that will help you remember information quickly and easily. Make sure your pictures are extremely clear, vivid and detailed, and in colour, and be sure to include strong actions in each picture. I can't emphasise enough the importance of action—it is the link between what you want to remember and your body part, and without it, it's very difficult to recall the relevant information.

In building your pictures, try to be as outrageous as possible; the stranger you make each situation, the more action you include, and the more of your senses (sight, smell, touch, hearing and taste) you include, the easier it is to recall. So don't restrict your pictures to what is possible in real life.

Remember, your mind thinks in pictures, so make each picture as stimulating to your mind as possible. The idea of 'linking' may seem a little strange at first, but the links are what holds everything in place and ensures that the information is there again when you need it.

Remembering names

The secret to remembering the names of the people you meet is simple, be interested in them—you must want to remember the information. Ask yourself how many times you have forgotten someone's name only minutes after meeting them— the reason is probably that you weren't paying attention to the other person in the first place.

The trick is to make sure that you're fully in the present moment. Most of the time, part of our mind is busy thinking of things we did yesterday or the things we have to do tomorrow, and we're only giving what is happening now a small amount of our concentration—and we still question why we can't remember what just happened! The challenge is not to allow your mind to drift away and focus on other things.

Pay attention when you're being introduced to someone. Focus on the person you're being introduced to and concentrate on really hearing their name. It's also important to use the person's name as soon and as often as possible—practising a name will help commit it to memory. Make a habit of using a person's name in all your conversations, because people love hearing their own name.

Paying attention to your immediate surroundings will help you file much more information in your short-term memory than you thought possible. Remember, your short-term memory is the filing drawer that stores your experiences that are anywhere from a few seconds to a few hours old. To help store the information in your long-term memory, all that's needed is to mix in a little emotion and action.

Remembering numbers

If you find it a little difficult to remember numbers, then you're not alone. The problem with numbers is that it's difficult to attach any emotion to them. And as you know, attaching emotion to something is the key to transferring information to your long-term memory—the filing drawer that contains the information you couldn't forget even if you wanted to. It's also difficult to connect images or pictures to numbers, and this is a problem, because your mind thinks about everything in pictures.

However, there is a simple way to remember the sets of numbers you need to know. In fact, you're probably using the technique already—it's called chunking. It's great for times when you need to remember a new telephone number. All you need to do is to break the number into smaller parts. For example, rather than trying to remember the long string 998451237, it's much easier for your mind to remember 99 84 51 237, or 9984 51237, or some other combination that you feel comfortable with.

Memory tips

* Relaxation is a great way to put you in the right state to absorb information. Being stressed will affect your ability to remember and also to recall information when you need it, so relax. The 'Power Learning' section in this chapter talks a little about the benefits of relaxation and some techniques to use.

∗ Improving how you breathe is easy and extremely effective. By improving how you breathe you will reduce your stress and increase the supply of oxygen to your brain and throughout your body.

∗ Listening to music will also aid your mind's ability to remember. Make sure that the music you listen to is close to the natural rhythm of your heart (sixty beats per minute), like baroque.

∗ Get a full night's sleep the night before you have to sit for an exam or give an important presentation. In fact, if you don't get a full night's rest, your ability to remember the information you've studied can drop by as much as thirty per cent. Also avoid the temptation to cram the night before—you won't remember the information anyway if you miss out on your sleep.

∗ Positive self-talk will not only improve your memory, but also your life. Stop believing that you have a terrible memory, and start believing in just how powerful it really is. Also, the more positive you are, the less stressed you'll be, and the less stressed you are the greater your ability to remember information.

∗ Exercising regularly increases the supply of oxygen to your brain. Oxygen is what fuels the brain and is important for both your short-term and long-term memory.

∗ Eating sensibly has a bigger effect on your memory that you probably realise. Not only does your brain need oxygen, it also needs the right kind of energy. What you eat effects your memory—you can't expect great results from your body or memory if you're feeding it rubbish. When you really need your memory to kick in, avoid over-eating—if your body isn't busy trying to digest large amounts of food, there will be more energy available for your brain to use.

* Alcohol is not kind to your brain so go easy on it.

* Take regular breaks when you're studying. Don't go beyond thirty minutes without stopping to recharge your body and mind. Taking a break for ten minutes or so will allow your mind to relax and to take in the information subconsciously.

Power Reading

When most people read, whether it be their favourite book or one they have to study, they let their eyes wander aimlessly, occasionally reading the same words or sentences more than once. This not only hinders how quickly you get through the information, but can also be frustrating. If this sounds familiar, you may want to consider the following techniques. The strength of these techniques lies in their simplicity, so don't doubt how effective they can be in helping to improve your reading speed. You'll notice huge improvements by making them a part of your everyday reading style.

The first step towards increasing your reading speed is to use your hand as a guide. Doing this has two major advantages—it will not only help guide your eyes through the information, but will also prevent you reading the same words and sentences over and over. When using your hand as a guide, there are two techniques to choose from. The first is to place your hand flat on the page, palm down, and focus on the words above your middle finger. The second technique is to use your pointer finger as a guide and to focus on the words directly above it. You'll need to experiment with each of these and find the one you're most comfortable with.

Once you've chosen where to focus, the next step is to scan each line from the left to the right side of the page. Remember to use your hand as your guide, making sure that your eyes follow. When you get to the end of each line, go back to the beginning of the next line and start again. It's that simple.

If you're reading the information for study purposes, a great timesaving tool is to read with a highlighter or marking pen in your hand and use the tip of the pen as your guide. You're not only increasing the speed at which you're reading but are also able to summarise the information at the same time, which will help when it comes to making notes to review.

Increasing your reading speed

In increasing your reading speed, it is important to trust that your mind knows what it's reading. It's not necessary to slow down to read difficult words or phrases, or to go over information that you think you missed the first time round. The trick to increasing your reading speed is to get your eyes used to scanning the information as quickly as possible. Practising the following exercise is a good way to condition your eyes. Like all exercises, the more you practise, the better the results.

* First, choose a passage to practise on.

* For the first twenty seconds, use your finger or highlighter as a guide and read as fast as you can while understanding the information.

* For the next twenty seconds, using your finger or highlighter as a guide, read the first half of the line, pause for a second, then scan the rest of the line. Move onto the next line and continue this technique until the twenty seconds is up.

* For the next twenty seconds, again using your highlighter or hand as a guide, read one third of the line, pause for a

second, then scan the rest of the line. Move onto the next line and continue this technique until the twenty seconds is up.

If you are interested in measuring your initial reading speed before you begin, read for ten seconds in your usual manner, without using your finger or highlighter as a guide. Then count the number of words you've just read and multiply it by six to determine your initial reading speed per minute. I'm sure you'll find it interesting to do this again after you've practised your new techniques for a week or so. Let your results be the judge.

Permission to judge a book by its cover

If you really want to increase the effectiveness of your reading, then take advantage of the information that is offered throughout a book. This means ignoring the old saying 'Don't judge a book by its cover' because the cover of a book and how it's laid out can save you many valuable hours. Many people read the majority of a book before realising that it isn't relevant or that it's just plain boring. To save you both time and effort, keep the following points in mind:

* The front and back cover of a book often tell you why the book was written and what you can expect from having read the book. The cover of a book is somewhat like a menu—it should be just enough to tempt and interest you, but leave you looking forward to the main meal.

* The introduction and 'About the Author' section explain the purpose of the book and the author's background. Understanding a little about the author will often bring the book to life for the reader. It will help you understand the context of the information—for example, what the author was thinking when the book was written, the circumstances

of the time-period in which it was written, and why certain things were included and others were not.

* The 'Table of Contents' gives you a good summary of all the information. It also directs you to the main subject areas, which means you can skip the information that is irrelevant or that you aren't interested in.

* Diagrams or tables throughout the book break up the information and make reading easier for you. And if a picture tells a thousand words, that means you'll need to do a lot less reading.

* Skimming through other sections, such as the index and glossary, will also give you a better understanding of the depth of the book. For example, if the glossary runs for pages and pages, chances are the book will be quite a heavy read.

Make these areas of a book your first priority; gaining an understanding of information before diving into it is an effective way to go about reading and research, especially when you are pressed for time. If after having read these sections of the book it still doesn't grab you, then it's likely you won't be any more interested in the book after you have read it.

Remember, The A.S.K. Key is your tuning key for life.

Step Three—Set Your Groove

This technique shows you how to develop a positive mental focus that will enable you to turn a negative state into a positive state. It can also be used as a relaxation technique that clears your mind, giving you a clean platform to work from.

More often then not, we let a single situation determine how our day will be, but by using Set Your Groove you can take charge of your feelings, deal with the situation and move on. The technique can be applied to all facets of your personal, business and sporting life. It can be used after receiving an upsetting phone call that would otherwise disrupt your whole day; when you are having a particularly bad game of sport and mentally want to throw the towel in or on a Monday morning when you are having trouble simply getting it together. Set Your Groove enables you to put a negative situation behind you and re-focus to give yourself a fresh start.

There are four simple steps involved in Setting Your Groove, and together they take less then one minute. You may be familiar with one or two of the techniques used here, but the real strength of Set Your Groove lies in combining the four steps into one technique.

1. Change focus

Focus away from your negative feeling by turning your attention to something totally unrelated. Whatever you choose to focus on, notice it in detail. Concentrate on it for ten to fifteen seconds. Changing your focus will break your state simply because it is only really possible to focus on one thing at a time.

2. Control your breathing

Your breathing actually changes in response to how you're feeling. For example, when you are anxious or upset your breathing becomes faster than normal and this affects your ability to make good decisions. Bring your breathing back to a comfortable pace that is normal for you, by taking three or four deep breaths and relaxing your body.

3. Visualisation

Close your eyes and see yourself completing the task at hand successfully. Make sure the picture is bright and clear. See and hear the scene in as much detail as possible—as if it's really happening. This should take no more than fifteen seconds.

4. Check your physiology

Make sure that your physiology is positive and supportive of the action you are about to take. You should find that in most cases this happens automatically after working through the first three steps. Take on the physiology of a winner—head up, shoulders back and standing confidently.

To illustrate how powerful Set Your Groove is, let's look at how it can be applied to a football team who have just had a try scored against them. Picture the team, waiting behind the goal posts for the opposition to convert the goal they have just scored. This time is usually spent in an extremely negative state of mind, so what we do with this time instead is to Set Your Groove:

Change focus   Rather than focusing on what went wrong and laying the blame on each other, each member changes their focus to something unrelated, like the number of people watching the game or the sponsorship signage around the field. Concentrating on something else is enough to break their current state of mind.

Control your breathing   While the team is waiting for the opposition to convert the try, the players take three or four deep breaths to bring their breathing back to normal and to eliminate those anxious feelings, and also to help them think more clearly.

Visualisation   At the same time, each of the players visualises their team scoring the next try. If a player has a problem visualising something in the future, then they can simply think back to a time when they felt positive, confident or powerful. It may have been a local golf contest that they won, or even watching their child win the under-twelves' running race.

Check your physiology   Before the team heads back for kick off, I have them stand like a team of champions—heads up, shoulders back, chests out and running powerfully back into the game. This usually throws the opposition right off—this team has just had a try scored against them, and possibly converted, yet they look like winners. The power of these four steps is huge.

Making these four steps part of how you operate gives you the same access to a powerful and positive state of mind from which to take the next step, so turn to whatever section you like and start your journey towards success and happiness now!

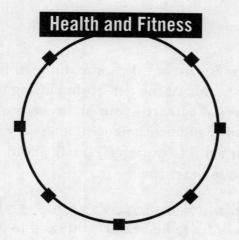

Health and Fitness

Optimum health and fitness is about ensuring that you pay attention to the foods, thoughts and activities you feed your mind and body on a daily basis.

Health and Fitness

Health and fitness are not the same thing. In fact, fitness is only a part of health. At the risk of simplifying things, fitness relates to physical activity—your ability to produce instant power with only a moment's notice. Fitness is generally measured by your aerobic capacity. I'll talk about this in more detail further into the chapter.

Health, on the other hand, relates to the overall wellness of your body. In order to be healthy you need to do more than just exercise. You need to feed your body with healthy foods, healthy thoughts and healthy activity. When you consider the example of a top-performing athlete you can see that the concept of attitude is like icing on a cake. Healthy thoughts, or a healthy attitude, often give an athlete the edge. It enables them to cut their time by just enough to make the difference between first and second place in a competition.

Your most important asset

You've probably heard it said before that without your health you have nothing. Well, it's true that your health is your single most important asset. If you are trying to excel in other areas of your life yet are unfit and unhealthy then it will be more than an uphill battle. It's like entering the Grand Prix in a Morris Minor.

There are three important factors that determine your level of health—your diet, your exercise, and your thoughts. It makes sense then that illness is a result of something you have eaten, something you have done or something you have thought. It sounds simple enough, but very few people understand how to improve their level of health and/or fitness. Rarely do they question the effects on their body of the foods that they eat, the thoughts that they have or the lack of exercise in their daily routine. Take a moment to answer these questions: are you feeding your body the right foods? Are you thinking positive thoughts? Are you exercising enough to strengthen your heart and body?

The human body is an awesome piece of machinery. If it is supplied with the right food, the right thoughts, and is exercised and allowed enough time to rest, it will function well. However, if it is treated poorly, it is likely to malfunction sooner or later.

This chapter is divided into two main sections. The first section looks at exercise and the benefits derived from it. The second part looks at the foods we eat to fuel our bodies so they can peak perform.

Part 1—Why exercise?

The purpose of exercising is to improve your metabolic rate (the number of kilojoules your body burns at any given moment)—to improve your circulation; to increase the level of oxygen in your blood (oxygen and water are the lifelines of your cells); to reduce stress and to decrease your risk of coronary heart disease. If your level of fitness is down there with the bottom twenty per cent of the population then you are sixty-five per cent more likely to die from cancer, a heart attack, stroke, or diabetes than those highly fit people in the top twenty per cent of the population. The good news is, that by taking a thirty-minute walk (about three kilometres), three to four times a week you decrease your risk of major disease dramatically. In fact, you are only ten per cent more likely to die of these major causes than those people in the top twenty per cent. Apart from the physical benefits of exercise, it is also great for your mind and your spirit. Exercising is a great way to increase your energy levels and to eliminate stress.

The human body remains an amazing piece of machinery into old age—eighty-year-olds are capable of doing the same things as forty-year-olds if their bodies are trained and conditioned to do so. Don't allow your age, or any other factor, to stop you from enjoying the benefits of exercising. And better still don't wait until you have had a serious health scare before you start making use of your body.

Assessing your fitness level

Before beginning an exercise routine, take the time to evaluate your fitness. If you are over forty, or if you have a prior medical condition or injury, it is best to visit your family doctor, or be assessed by a fitness professional. Assessing your fitness level before jumping into an exercise program can save you a lot of time and heartache later on.

Fitness level definitions

As a starting point in determining your level of fitness, consider these four categories, ranging from a beginner through to an expert. Although there may be some overlap, the definitions are helpful in determining how you should exercise.

Beginners   You belong to this category if you never do any exercise or you are over forty years of age.

Intermediate   You have exercised on and off during the past year.

Advanced   You exercise at least three to four times a week on a regular basis.

Expert   Your lifestyle is heavily based on sport, or you are a professional sports person.

There are various other measurements that will give you important information about your physical condition, including your heart rate, strength, flexibility and body fat. With this information you can decide on what you'd like to achieve from your exercise program and how best to achieve it.

Heart rate

Your heart rate, also referred to as your pulse-rate, is the number of times your heart beats in one minute. Being able to monitor your heart rate before, during and after exercising is essential in making sure that you are working at the correct level of intensity for your body.

One of the most effective ways of monitoring your heart rate is by measuring your pulse, and although it can be a little tricky at first, it will become second nature by practising the correct technique a few times. The best time to measure your heart rate is first thing in the morning, just after getting out of bed.

You can take your pulse in one of two places—on the side of your neck, or on your wrist—I prefer the first method. Here's what to do:

1. Using the first two fingers of your right hand, start from your right ear and follow under your jaw-line until you come to the muscle running down your neck. You should be able to feel the throb under your fingertips.

2. Press down gently.

3. When you have found your pulse, count the number of pulses for ten seconds.

4. Multiply it by six. This figure is your heart rate.

Resting Pulse Rate

Age	Poor	Fair	Good	Excellent
Men				
20–29	86+	70–84	62–68	60 or less
30–39	86+	72–84	64–70	62 or less
40–49	90+	74–88	66–72	64 or less
50+	90+	76–88	68–74	66 or less
Women				
20–29	96+	78–94	72–76	70 or less
30–39	98+	80–96	72–78	70 or less
40–49	100+	80–98	74–78	72 or less
50+	104+	84–102	76–82	74 or less

To take your pulse at your wrist follow these steps: place your middle and index fingertips on your opposite wrist, right under the base of your thumb. You may be able to see your radial artery—the thin blue line showing through your skin. Count the number of beats for ten seconds, and then multiply the figure by six to give you the number of beats per minute.

Generally, women have a higher heart rate than men; anything up to ten beats per minute more. This is because the female heart is smaller, and because females usually carry more fat than men to protect their reproductive organs. You'll find that as your fitness improves, your heart rate will decrease—by exercising you will increase your heart's efficiency and it will need to beat less times per minute to pump blood throughout your body.

Maximum heart rate

Your maximum heart rate is literally your heart's maximum capacity for pumping blood. Your heart rate increases the harder you work, but as with most things, there are limits beyond which it is unsafe to push yourself. Determining your maximum heart rate is one way to gauge the maximum level of intensity that you can safely work to.

To calculate your maximum heart rate, all you need to do is subtract your age from 220. If you are thirty-five years old then your heart rate at maximum exertion should be about 185 (220–35).

Your target heart rate

Finding the right balance between pushing too hard and being too easy on yourself is important if you are to benefit from your exercise routine. Your Target Heart Rate (THR), or Target Training Zone (TTZ), is a mid-range level of exertion and is usually between fifty and eighty-five per cent of your maximum heart rate. Calculating your THR is simple.

Calculate your maximum heart rate by deducting your age from 220.

$$220 - 35 = 185$$

Multiply your maximum heart rate by 0.5 to estimate the low end of your target zone.

$$185 \times 0.5 = 92.5$$

Let's say 93. Multiply your maximum heart rate by 0.85 to estimate the high end of your target zone.

$$185 \times 0.85 = 157.25$$

Let's say 158.

The area between 93 beats per minute and 158 beats per minute is the range that you should work within when you are exercising. If you fall below 93 beats per minute then you need to work harder, and if you go above 158 beats per minute you need to ease back. If you are a beginner, then it's best to sit at the lower end of your target zone until you improve your fitness. This will allow you to work out longer with a lower chance of injury.

Recovery rate

Your recovery rate determines how long it takes your heart to slow down after exercising and is generally measured thirty seconds after having exercised. Count your pulse for ten seconds and multiply it by six. Now compare your results to the Recovery Rate Pulse Chart. It's a good idea to monitor your recovery rate to measure your improvement. You'll find that your heart rate will drop faster as your level of fitness increases.

Recovery Pulse Rate After 30 Seconds

Age	Poor	Fair	Good	Excellent
Men				
20–29	102+	86–100	76–84	74 or less
30–39	102+	88–100	80–86	78 or less
40–49	106+	90–104	82–88	80 or less
50+	106+	92–104	84–90	82 or less
Women				
20–29	112+	94–110	88–92	86 or less
30–39	114+	96–112	88–94 ,	86 or less
40–49	116+	96–114	90–94	88 or less
50+	118+	100–116	92–98	90 or less

Fill In Your Own Pulse Rates

Rate Taken	Maximum	Target	Initial Recovery
Now			
In 3 months			
In 6 months			

Talk test

The 'talk test' is another method that can be used to determine the level of intensity you are exercising at—it's a straightforward way to determine if you are working too hard or being too easy on yourself. It is a simple and effective method: while exercising you should be able to speak in short sentences, but not be able to carry out a full conversation. If you can't manage to speak using short sentences then you are probably exercising harder than you need to, and at a greater intensity than necessary for safe training. If you are a beginner, don't continue to exercise at this level. The opposite also applies—you know you are being too easy on yourself if there is no difficulty in talking while exercising. You should feel like there is effort involved and that you are working, but not that you are about to collapse.

Weighing it all up

Carrying excess weight is placing extra pressure on your body that it just doesn't need. You are not doing yourself any favours by hanging onto those extra kilos. In fact, take a look around and count the number of people that are fat and over seventy years old—I'm sure you won't find too many people that fit this description.

However, just weighing yourself is of limited value, simply because your weight can be misleading. Muscle weighs more than fat, and when you compare two people of the same height and weight the results can be surprising. Let me explain.

Person A is an unfit office worker. He is six feet tall and weighs 110 kg. He rarely exercises and has a very high body-fat measurement. Person B is the same height and weight, but is a top athlete with a lot of muscle and a low body-fat measurement. What's interesting is that both Person A and Person B weigh the same, yet their physical appearances and condition couldn't be more different.

Body-fat percentage

Because your weight alone can be misleading, it is helpful to know your body composition, or your body-fat percentage. Although the measurement is not exact, it will give you an idea of how much of your body is fat, and how much is lean body tissue. This test can be done by your doctor, an instructor at the local gymnasium or by a Personal Trainer.

If you score twenty-two per cent on a fat test this means that twenty-two per cent of your total weight is fat. For women, the ideal score is between sixteen and twenty-six per cent. For men, their ideal body-fat measurement is somewhere between twelve and eighteen per cent. However, don't get caught up on this measurement alone—let the mirror be the judge. Be honest and realistic and keep in mind that your ultimate goal should be improving your level of health and fitness so you can enjoy life more fully.

Once you have assessed your level of fitness using these measurements, you can then go on to develop some personal goals relating to your training and what you want to achieve.

What are your goals?

Reaching an increased level of health and fitness will be much easier if you know what you actually want to achieve. Determining why you want to make the improvements will provide you with the direction you need—consider it your road map for reaching your destination. Ask yourself why you want to improve your health and fitness.

Maybe you are fed up with not having enough energy to do the things you want to do. Or perhaps you are finding it more difficult to keep up with your children. Or you are simply tired of carrying around that extra weight. Take some time now to determine your reasons for wanting to make the improvement, keeping in mind that your goal should be to improve the quality of your life.

Once you have done this you can then set yourself some short, medium and long-term goals. Setting these different goals will make it easier to achieve your overall goal. Remember to be realistic, and set small goals for yourself to achieve. Setting only one major goal can be disheartening—it may be such a big ask that you lose interest and inspiration. Try setting smaller goals that add up to achieving the larger one. This approach is much more motivating, especially if you reward yourself along the way.

For more information on the importance of goal setting and how to set goals that produce results, have a read through the chapter on goal setting.

Short-term goals

Your short-term goals refer to the things you want to achieve by the end of your exercise session, or the end of each day or week. They may include eating a low-fat lunch, or working out for thirty minutes on the walking machine, or reading an article on the correct way to stretch.

Medium-term goals

Your medium-term goals are things that you want to achieve within one week to three months. Maybe you want to improve your heart rate, or improve the time it takes to walk two kilometres, or increase the number of times you work out per week from three to four sessions. Medium-term goals will help maintain your level of motivation, and should act as stepping stones in achieving your long-term goal.

Long-term goals

When setting long-term goals, allow three to six months to achieve them. It's important to be realistic in setting these goals—don't under-estimate yourself, but be careful not to set goals that you have no chance of achieving. Setting goals that are beyond your reach can cause you to lose motivation. And remember, you can adjust your goals if you need to; it's all part of fine-tuning your life. Some examples of long-term goals include losing ten kilos in fifteen weeks; being able to walk two kilometres in twenty minutes; or entering—and completing—a local fun run.

Maintaining the motivation to reach your ultimate goal may at times be a little testing. A simple tool to combat this is to reward yourself along the way. Each time that you achieve a short, medium and long-term goal, treat yourself to something special—it may be the latest music CD, a trip to see a block-buster movie or a new book. Whatever you decide, make sure that it doesn't go against your ultimate goal—rewarding your-self with a block of chocolate or two weeks off training isn't quite the idea.

How to be a stayer, not a player

Here's a statistic for you: within eight weeks of starting a new exercise program fifty per cent of people quit. You can con-gratulate yourself then if you are one of the fifty per cent who stick with it, and if you haven't quite made it past the first eight weeks, then read on.

The main reason people quit exercising is because of bore-dom. If you become a little bored with your routine, try some-thing different. Instead of swimming, go for a walk, or instead of running try cycling. You might want to change your routine every month or so. You'll find that by trying a variety of exercises, your motivation and interest will remain high.

Another way to maintain your motivation is by training with a friend. There will be mornings when you won't feel like jumping out of bed, but if it means letting yourself and your training partner down then you'll be much more inclined to make the effort. You'll be surprised at how much you can achieve when you are spurred on by a partner. If you can't find a friend to train with, then consider joining a fitness club. One word of warning, however, when training with a partner: don't compare yourself with them, or anyone else for that matter. Keep in mind that your shape and body composition is unique. Do the best that you can, and measure your achievements by your own goals and your ability to achieve them.

Any new kind of exertion you put on your body is going to take some effort. You can't expect to achieve your goals without an increased level of effort and commitment, especially if you haven't exercised for a while. However, having the right equipment will make it much easier on your body. If your routine includes walking, then invest in a good pair of walking shoes—the initial investment is a worthwhile one. You don't have to go out and buy top of the range equipment, but make sure that it is adequate for your needs.

To make exercising a part of your daily routine, train at the same time, and on the same days of the week, so exercising becomes a habit. Remember you are only human—if your motivation sways, or you stop exercising for a short while, that's OK. The important thing is to accept what's happened and make a commitment to start again. Another tip in staying motivated is to …

Know what works

For many people, exercising can be somewhat hit-and-miss. They set out on an exercise program but never monitor or evaluate how effective their training is. This is where keeping a training log is useful.

Start by writing down every exercise that you do on a daily basis. This way, you will know what exercises are helping you achieve your goals. It won't be a matter of trying to guess what is working and what isn't. Keeping a training log will also give you an idea of how realistic and achievable your goals are. It can also be motivating to look back on what you achieved over the week. It may even inspire you to do more the following week.

The rules of exercising have changed

The rules of exercising have changed, and this is great news— it's no longer necessary to do a heavy, strenuous workout six or seven days a week. In fact, excessive exercise can actually be bad for you. Today, it is more a case of moderate exercise as few as three to four times a week, for thirty minutes each session. To make it even simpler, you don't have to exercise for a solid thirty minutes—three lots of ten-minute blocks will have the same effect.

You may be surprised to know that even getting out of your seat to change the television channel instead of using the remote, or using the stairs instead of the lift, or walking to the corner store instead of jumping in the car, all make a difference—any activity is better than no activity. Although …

The magic exercise—walking

Simply walking to the bus stop or train station each morning and afternoon is not enough in itself, although it is better than being totally inactive. To have any significant impact on your fitness, the exercise you do must get you at least lightly puffing.

I'm a big fan of walking—it is one of the best exercises that you can do if you walk fast enough to build up a sweat. You'll need to walk three to four times a week, from two to six kilometres each time. To give you an idea of how much time you should spend walking, each kilometre should take approximately ten minutes.

Fast walking is definitely underrated as a form of aerobic exercise. It is great for everyone, especially those who have problems with running and other high-impact exercises. Walking puts minimum strain on your muscles and joints, and this of course means that you are less likely to injure yourself.

Another benefit is that walking costs nothing—all you need is a pair of good shoes—and of course the motivation to start. That's the beauty of walking—it can start you on an exercise program that will give you the results you're after, and if you need a little push, you can start walking with a training partner—you'll find that you'll motivate each other, which means you'll achieve your goals sooner. So find some nice places to walk—through the park or along the beach—and vary your routine so you don't become bored. You should aim to increase either the distance you walk, or improve your time, and keep in mind that the harder you work the more your overall fitness will improve.

Now, in developing your exercise program there are four principles that you should consider. They are frequency, intensity, time and type. They are also known as ...

The F.I.T.T. Principle

Frequency   Frequency refers to the number of sessions you exercise. You should aim to exercise at least three times per week, and rest every other day. The days you rest are just as important because your body needs time to recover and adapt to the added demands you are placing on it.

Intensity   Intensity is the amount of effort you put into your workout. To achieve the results you want, your body must work harder than normal to generate overload. The best indication of whether you are working hard enough to improve your fitness is by measuring your Target Training Zone (TTZ). This is based on training at between fifty to eighty-five per cent of your maximum heart rate.

Time   Time refers to the duration of each session. You should exercise for a minimum of thirty minutes. Keep in mind that the intensity of exercise is more important than the duration—many people spend too much time exercising at an intensity that is too low to improve their fitness.

Type   Type is simply the kind of exercise you choose to do. This will depend on your fitness goals, but the most beneficial type of training is aerobic.

Aerobic and anaerobic exercise

There are two types of exercise—aerobic and anaerobic.

Aerobic exercise

Aerobic exercise means exercise 'with oxygen'—exercise where you are able to breathe easily to produce the energy you need. For example, walking, running, swimming, cycling and dancing where the exercise can be maintained for long periods of time. There are many benefits associated with aerobic exercise—here are just a few:

* an increased lung capacity—your lungs are able to process more air with less effort

* a stronger heart—this means your heart can pump more blood in fewer strokes

* an increased blood supply to your muscles

* an ability to eliminate waste products more efficiently

* an increased ability to digest your food.

In short, your body will feel alive, healthy and fit!

Anaerobic exercise

Anaerobic means 'without oxygen'. With this type of exercise, your body uses oxygen at a faster rate than it can be supplied. This means that your body creates energy even without oxygen. However, you can only keep this up for a very short time before your body is forced to return to aerobic exercise. You may have seen an athlete sprint a short distance using a sudden burst of energy—this is a good example of anaerobic activity. Keep in mind that this type of exercise is not part of an ordinary fitness program.

Flexibility and the importance of stretching

Flexibility is a measurement of how far and how easily you can move your joints and the muscles attached to them. The older we become, the more our muscles shorten and tighten. As a result, our bodies become less flexible, and this restricts the way we function. If your joints and muscles are inflexible, then your level of flexibility is considered tight.

The best way to improve your flexibility is through stretching. This is a matter of loosening and lengthening those muscles that have become a little stiff and shorter with age and/or under-use. By increasing your flexibility you'll be able to carry out a fuller range of movements and your recovery period after training will be shortened.

There are a number of other benefits that come from stretching—it helps you relax, prevents injury, increases your blood circulation, reduces tension in your muscles and increases your general mobility. Flexibility is not only important in exercise and sport, but also in general day-to-day activities.

There are stretches that can be done for almost every muscle in your body, so don't limit your stretching to one or two areas. However, you will get the best results by concentrating your stretching on the muscles that you plan to exercise.

The best time to stretch is both before and after exercising. Stretching before you work out helps warm up and prepare your muscles for exercise, and stretching afterwards helps loosen and lengthen your muscles and speed up their recovery time.

When it comes to stretching, there are a number of things to keep in mind. Perhaps most importantly, don't overdo it. If you over-exert your muscles they will shorten rather than lengthen and this will tighten the muscle rather than loosen it. Gradually lengthen the muscle by holding it in a stretched position for between ten and thirty seconds. You'll know when you are stretching correctly because you'll feel a slight tension in the muscle. The tension should be slight—if there is pain involved then ease off a little. And never bounce while stretching. Achieving your desired flexibility may take some time so be patient. You'll find that on some days you are more flexible than others, so listen to your body and stretch and work out accordingly.

Make the most of any opportunity you have to stretch—have a stretch any time of the day, perhaps in the car waiting for traffic, or at your desk to get your blood circulating again. You'll feel great afterwards.

Warming up

Warming up prepares your body for a workout—it gets your cardiovascular system working efficiently and loosens and frees the joints by increasing the temperature in your muscles and the tissue around them. When your muscles are warm they are less likely to tear, simply because they are more flexible. Warming up also helps direct the blood to where it will be most needed for your workout. Despite the importance of warming up, many people overlook it as part of their exercise routine. Don't be tempted to skip your warm-up, even if you are pushed for time—if you do your chances of injury will increase considerably. If you haven't exercised for quite a while and are out of shape, then warming up is even more important. Keep in mind that the longer you plan to work out, the longer your warm-up session should be.

Before jumping into your workout, spend between five and fifteen minutes doing some kind of light aerobic exercise such as walking, cycling or jogging, increasing your resting pulse rate to between forty and fifty per cent of your maximum heart rate. As you exercise, you can increase your rate to somewhere between sixty and eighty-five per cent, but don't go beyond this. You don't have to over-exert yourself to gain the full benefit of exercising. All you need to do is reach a level of exertion where you are lightly puffing.

Cooling down

Cooling down after having exercised is just as important as warming up—in fact, both warming up and cooling down should be an essential part of your exercise routine. The purpose of cooling down is to reduce your body temperature, to redirect the flow of blood evenly throughout your body, and to slow your heart to its normal rate.

Many people finish their routine suddenly, and this sends their body into shock. This causes blood to pool in their veins, and their muscles to contract. This can have a number of effects, including dizziness, nausea, fainting, lactic acid build up (where the muscles feel heavy and stiff) and a general loss of flexibility.

When you have finished your workout, rather than stopping suddenly, slow down gradually using the same exercise you did to warm up, be it jogging, walking or cycling. Again, spend between five and ten minutes cooling down, even longer if your workout was really tough. Eliminating the warming up and cooling down part of a routine are two of the major causes of injury.

How to avoid injury

Unfortunately, for many people injury seems to go hand in hand with exercising. As soon as they begin to put extra demands on their body, the chances of incurring an injury increase. However, this doesn't have to be the case—while you can't eliminate the risk of injury altogether, you can minimise it. Part of the answer is to understand how your body works, and to work out accordingly. Listen to your body while exercising and take note of what it is trying to tell you.

Prevention is always better than cure, so to avoid injury, it may be helpful to know some of the most common causes. They include:

* not warming up and cooling down

* not stretching both before and after exercising

* inadequate rest between workouts

* working out too often

* poor technique

* not listening to your body

* not working within your limitations

* bad habits, including smoking, drinking, and drugs

* poor eating habits—incorrect and inadequate intake

The good news is that these traps can be easily avoided and the correct approaches can be simply incorporated into your exercise routine.

Acute and chronic injury

If you do injure yourself, it will help to know whether your injury is acute or chronic. An acute injury will give you a sudden intense pain, or a loss of power. If the injury stops you from doing a certain movement for between twenty-four and forty-eight hours, then it is an acute injury.

A chronic injury on the other hand, is one that lasts for days, weeks, or even months if you are particularly unlucky. It is an injury that wants to stick around, even if you are treating and resting it.

How to treat an injury

What you do within the first twenty-four hours after an injury will affect the seriousness of your injury and determine the recovery time. When an injury occurs, the area grows inflamed, usually becoming hot, red, swollen and painful. The extent of the inflammation will vary from injury to injury, so it's important that you do all you can to slow the inflammation. There's an easy way to remember how to do this; it's called P.R.I.C.E.D.

P.R.I.C.E.D.

Prevention   Prevention is better than cure—stretch, warm-up and cool down.

Rest   Resting the injured area for at least twenty-four to forty-eight hours is the best treatment. Many people think that they can work through their injury—this will only make the injury worse. Although the pain may subside, the damage will increase—the swelling and bleeding will spread, making the injured area more vulnerable to further injury.

Ice   Apply an icepack for between fifteen and twenty minutes every two hours for at least twenty-four hours after the injury is sustained.

Compression   Use elastic bandages to limit the flow of fluids—this will help reduce swelling and internal bleeding. Make sure the bandages are not too tight.

Elevation   Elevate the injured area above your heart—this will reduce the blood flow and will allow the fluids produced by the swelling or bleeding to drain away.

Diagnosis   You'll have a much better chance of early recovery the earlier your injury is seen to by a doctor or physiotherapist.

Muscles and weight training

The ability of your muscles to sustain and complete a certain movement against resistance is determined by your strength. The advantage of having strong muscles is twofold—they help support your skeleton and keep your body upright. So what is a muscle, and how does it work?

A muscle is a collection of fibres connected to your bones by your tendons. Although there are approximately 600 muscles in our body, only around eighty are used for exercise. The size and shape of muscles is quite varied—they can measure anything from one to sixty millimetres in length.

When you are exercising, your muscles increase in size because of the extra blood flowing through them. This is sometimes referred to as 'pump'; it's much the same as pumping up a tyre. However, the 'pump' effect is only temporary—when you stop exercising, the blood flow lessens and your muscles decrease in size.

Your muscles don't develop while you are working out—they actually develop after you have finished exercising, while you're resting. Your body also replenishes its energy levels at the same time. The heavier the weights and the longer you work out, the longer it takes for your muscles to recover.

You'll find you need less rest between workouts as your fitness improves. However, the minimum amount of time between workouts should be twenty-four hours. In increasing your muscle size, the rest time between workouts is as important as the exercising itself. Your muscle tissue needs time to repair and rebuild, and the only way it can do this is by taking advantage of the rest times between working out.

If your goal is to build muscle and gain strength, it's necessary to gradually increase the weights you are lifting. This gradual increase allows your body the time it needs to handle the extra demand. Sure, lifting more weights than you are used to will give your muscles a 'pump', but it will also tire your muscles, causing them to fatigue.

Each time your body reaches a new level of strength, it's important to increase the weight you are lifting or to work out more often—your body will respond with further muscle growth. The important thing is to not overload your body too quickly, but to progress gradually. Your body must be able to adapt and change without stress, and this means that your exercises and equipment must allow for small increases in weight. And remember, doing too much too soon could cause injury, which may stop you training and exercising altogether.

A good principle to keep in mind is that it's better to lift less weight with the correct exercise movement than more weight using a bad movement. The key factor is the way you use the weight, not the amount of weight you use.

Now, some people take the easy way out and only do the exercises they like, or find easy. The advantage is that they enjoy their workout, but the downside is that only certain muscle groups are being exercised. Make an effort to work on all your muscle groups so they grow in proportion, maintaining your body symmetry and improving your overall appearance.

A good eating plan is also extremely important when weight training. When you are training your body uses more energy, and that energy needs to come from the food you eat. Eating plenty of fruit, vegetables, bread and pasta will provide all the complex carbohydrates your body needs as fuel.

Excessive amounts of protein are not needed to build muscle. A balanced diet will give you all the protein you need to increase the size and strength of your muscles, so there's no need to make a deliberate point of eating excess quantities of it. You'll also find that protein-rich food piles on more fat than complex carbohydrates. I'll talk about the value of different types of food in Part 2 of this chapter.

Weight training has traditionally been associated with strong body-builders lifting exceptionally heavy weights in order to really 'bulk up'. When most people think of weight training the picture of Arnold Schwarzenegger usually comes to mind. However, it's not just the Arnold types that are lifting weights these days. Even seventy and eighty year olds are including some form of weight training in their routine, and for very good reasons too—lifting light weights will leave you feeling more healthy, fit, energetic and powerful.

Weight training also helps you maintain your strength as you get older. If you don't use your muscles they will waste away. This decline in your overall strength can begin from the time you are in your mid-twenties. If you don't exercise your muscles you can expect to lose thirty to forty-five per cent of your strength by the time you are sixty-five.

Weight training will also help keep your bones healthy. Osteoporosis is a debilitating disease affecting both men and women, in which the bone becomes porous and fragile. When your bones are weak they are more prone to fractures, the most common being hip, back and wrist. Weight training alone will not prevent bone loss, but it can help greatly. Again, it's a case of use it or lose it. If you don't place demands on your bones then there is no reason for them to stay strong. The more weight you are able to lift, the more stress you are able to put on your bones and it is this stress that stimulates them.

Weight training will also improve your appearance by firming, building, lifting and shaping your muscles. You can choose certain areas of your body that you would like to improve and/or emphasise and reshape them through weight training. Don't be fooled, however, into thinking that you can get rid of fat from a particular part of your body—there is no such thing as spot reduction.

Weight training also helps prevent injury—your muscles are less prone to injury if they are strong. Weight training can also be beneficial when it comes to losing weight because it increases your metabolism. Muscles also burn more kilojoules than fat does. Keep in mind that muscle weighs more than fat, so don't be alarmed if the scales show that your weight has increased.

The importance of water

More than seventy per cent of the human body is made up of water. In fact, every cell in your body needs water (and oxygen) to function properly. For this reason it's important to get enough water, particularly when you are exercising. As a rule of thumb, aim to drink eight cups (two litres) of water each day and up to twelve or thirteen if you are exercising.

If you think that drinking eight cups of water a day is excessive, then take a look at the reasoning. Each day you lose approximately ten cups of water from your body—it takes about six cups per day to remove the waste from your body; two cups are needed for breathing, and sweating and evaporation account for the other two.

When it comes to replenishing your water supply, it is possible to replace up to two cups with the water content of the food that you eat daily, if you eat water-rich foods like fruits and vegetables. However, you're still eight cups short and the best way to make up for this shortfall is simply to drink a minimum of eight cups of water each day.

Forming this habit may be a little difficult at first, so start by keeping a glass of water or a water bottle beside you throughout the day. Increasing the amount of water you drink will be much easier if you don't have to go out of your way to get it. And don't wait until you are thirsty, because being thirsty means that you are already dehydrated. If you have ever drunk too much alcohol you will know all about this effect.

Dehydration

When you exercise your body produces extra heat. For your body to function normally, it must get rid of any excess heat, and it does this by sweating. To give you an idea of just how easy it is to become dehydrated, consider this—if you work out for one hour, you'll lose approximately one litre of fluid. If you are cycling or running, you can lose up to two litres in one hour. The amount can be higher if you are exercising in hot or humid weather.

Dehydration occurs if you continue working out without replacing the fluid your body has lost. Being thirsty, either before or during exercise, means that your body is already dehydrated. When you sweat, you not only lose water, but also salt from your body. Take the time to re-hydrate your body with a glass of unsweetened fruit juice diluted with water, and add a pinch of salt. By adding salt to your re-hydration drink you are replacing the potassium, magnesium, and sodium—or salt—lost during exercise. This replacement is important for your muscles and nerves to function properly. Exercising while you are dehydrated only makes your workout more difficult, meaning you'll run out of energy sooner.

Part 2—Energy

Energy refers to the number of kilojoules or calories released when food is burned by the body. Of course, your body needs energy simply to keep you alive—your heart, muscles, kidneys, lungs, brain and other vital organs are all working twenty-four hours a day and are also undergoing constant repair. However, many people consume more kilojoules than their bodies need to carry out these tasks and the extra is stored as fat.

What do we mean by metabolic rate or metabolism?

Your metabolic rate, or metabolism, refers to the total number of kilojoules your body burns at any given time. When most people talk about metabolism, or metabolic rate, they are usually referring to their resting metabolism—the number of kilojoules their body needs to perform the basic functions mentioned above. An average person's metabolism will use approximately 6000 kilojoules of energy each day.

Your metabolic rate, to some extent, is determined by your genetics—some people are lucky and burn kilojoules quickly, while for others the reverse is true. Your metabolism is also determined by age—generally, the older you get, the slower your metabolism becomes. However, it is possible to boost your metabolic rate through aerobic exercises like jogging, swimming, and cycling. Keep in mind that if you get older and don't increase your level of exercise, you will store the energy your body doesn't need as fat.

The benefits of including exercise in your daily routine are twofold—you burn kilojoules while exercising, and because exercising increases your metabolic rate, you will also burn more kilojoules throughout the day—this is the most effective and safest way of losing weight. What many people fail to realise is that by dramatically restricting their food intake they are actually doing themselves an injustice. Your body's natural response to a sudden decrease in the amount of food it receives is to slow your metabolic rate, so the energy from the food you are eating can go further. Restricting your food intake is ineffective if you are trying to lose weight, because it will actually slow down your body's metabolic rate.

One thing I recommend is to eliminate the word 'diet' from your vocabulary. It has many negative connotations associated with it—depriving yourself of certain foods, counting the kilojoules and grams of fat that are in the foods you eat, feelings of guilt if you slip up and severely restricting the amount of food you eat.

Most people fail to lose weight and keep it off on a long-term basis when they go on a diet simply because of the way the body functions. When you lose weight quickly you lose fluid, fat and muscle, and the faster you lose weight the more muscle you lose. The problems begin when you stop dieting and return to your old eating patterns—the first thing you'll put back on is fluid, then fat, and then (if at all) muscle. However, you won't put on as much muscle as before, especially if you lose weight quickly. So the result is that you end up with more body fat than you had before you started your diet.

Another problem with dieting is that you eat less food than usual. As a result, you experience a loss of energy, which means that you have little or no motivation to exercise and you quit exercising altogether. A much healthier approach is to change how you think about food and to include exercise in your routine.

A healthy eating plan

The food you eat plays an important part in determining your level of health. Food provides your body with the fuel it needs to produce energy. It also provides the nutrients needed by the body to repair tissues and to grow. Your body is unable to carry out these tasks successfully if you base your diet on junk food. However, the opposite is also true—your body will perform better and last longer if you feed it well.

A healthy eating plan does not have to be boring, complicated, or bland. In fact, many healthy foods are delicious and easy to prepare, so invest in a healthy cookbook and have some fun— and keep in mind that a healthy eating plan is a balanced one. This means eating more of some foods and less of others.

There are many benefits that come from a healthy eating plan, but perhaps the most significant is the amount of energy you will have. Rather than arriving home at the end of each day and collapsing on the sofa, you'll find that your level of enthusiasm and energy will start to peak. You'll feel strong, healthy and alive. You'll also look younger, have a stronger immune system, and be better equipped to cope with stress.

Positive and negative foods

Why do you eat? The answer for many people is because food tastes good. However, the purpose of eating is really to supply your body and mind with the energy and fuel that it needs to keep you alive. A simple way to determine whether the food you are eating is beneficial for you is by grouping foods according to the effect they have on your body—think of foods as either 'positive foods' or 'negative foods'.

Positive Foods	Negative Foods
vegetables, fruit, grains, pasta, legumes, seafood, cereals, bread, rice. Also, to a lesser extent: chicken, turkey, nuts, eggs, dairy products	anything that doesn't fall into the positive group: chocolate, ice-cream, sweets, chips, foods that are high in sugars, salt and fat

It is more difficult for our bodies to deal with processed or negative foods than natural or positive foods. Our bodies are designed to run their best on positive foods—we are made to digest and make use of natural foods like fruits and vegetables, not negative foods like chocolate and cakes. Positive foods have the right quantities of nutrients, vitamins and minerals that we need to develop and maintain a healthy body. However, most negative foods have next to no nutrients, vitamins or minerals, but instead are packed with fat and sugar.

Of course, the idea is not to be fanatical and exclude all negative foods from your life, but to find a balance that makes you feel great. As a general rule, start by basing eighty per cent of your diet on positive foods and the other twenty per cent on negative foods. You'll find that as your level of health and fitness start to improve, your body will tell you what food it wants and needs in order to perform at its peak. You will probably find that the ratio will be more like ninety to ten per cent of positive foods to negative foods. You'll be surprised at your change in attitude and the way you swing towards positive foods as your body realises the benefits of a healthy eating plan.

Unfortunately, many people are not aware of the effects that certain foods have on their bodies, or that what they are putting into their bodies can be harmful. You have to take responsibility for your own health and fitness, and make a decision to feed your body and mind with the fuel that it needs to perform at its peak. If you don't, it will be difficult to excel in other areas of life.

Let's take a closer look at the foods we eat.

Food—your body's fuel

'You are what you eat'. I'm sure you've heard this before, but have you taken the time to consider just what it means? Many people have trouble applying it on a daily basis. Understanding that your body can only be as good as the food you supply it with is an important factor in providing your body with a balanced approach to eating.

Eating properly is essential to improve your level of health and fitness. It is also essential in developing and following a training program, simply because the energy you need comes from the food you put into your body.

The foods we eat provide our bodies with the nutrients, or fuel we need to function on a daily basis. Any of the nutrients that your body can use are absorbed into the bloodstream to be distributed through the body. Anything that your body cannot use is eliminated and any useable substances left over are stored by your body as fat.

Most of the foods we eat are a mixture of carbohydrates, proteins, and fats, along with vitamins, minerals, and water. Food is grouped together in these categories depending on the nutrients found in them.

Carbohydrates

Carbohydrates are your body's main source of fuel and are burned by the body and brain to provide energy. Your body will use carbohydrates as fuel before it uses protein and fat. In fact, for some types of physical activity, carbohydrates are the only source of fuel that your body is able to use. However, not all carbohydrates are equal.

There are two kinds of carbohydrates—simple and complex. Simple carbohydrates, or simple sugars, are man-made and contain no vitamins or minerals. They are found in processed foods and table sugar, like chocolate, cakes, biscuits and soft drinks. They consist of a single glucose molecule. This means that they are absorbed quickly into the bloodstream, giving you short, sudden bursts of energy. However, the sugar level in your blood will drop again suddenly, often leaving you feeling tired and hungry. Complex carbohydrates on the other hand are low in fat, low in kilojoules, and high in fibre. These are the good guys. They are found in foods like fruit, vegetables, pasta, legumes, grains, bread, cereals, rice and flour. Complex carbohydrates consist of hundreds of glucose molecules—this means that the sugar in complex carbohydrates is broken down and absorbed slowly by your body. So unlike simple carbohydrates, complex carbohydrates provide you with sustained energy, and leave you feeling full for a long time.

Simple carbohydrates, or simple sugars, are also found in fruit. There is, however, a difference between the sugars found in fruit and those in processed foods. The simple sugars found in fruit also come with loads of vitamins, minerals, fibre, and water—you won't find these in chocolate or soft drinks.

Proteins

Proteins are the building blocks of the body. Your skin, hair, nails, veins, bones, blood cells, tendons, muscles, arteries, enzymes and hormones are made of protein.

Proteins are made up of amino acids, and these amino acids are used by the body to build and repair damaged tissue. To carry out these actions, your body needs twenty different amino acids. It can produce some of these by itself, but the others have to come from the food that you eat. Nuts, seeds, eggs, lean meat, chicken, turkey, yogurt, fish, cheese, and milk are all good sources of protein. If you are not keen on dairy products, then try dried peas and beans, soya products, or lentils. There are many choices, even for vegetarians.

Fats

Experts suggest that fat should not account for more then twenty to thirty per cent of the total number of kilojoules we consume each day, but unfortunately fat makes up a large part of the Western diet. In saying this, it is important to understand that some fat in your diet is essential—fat is used for providing your body with fuel, in absorbing certain vitamins, keeping your skin moist and your joints lubricated and for keeping your immune system healthy. However, too much fat is dangerous—it increases your risk of heart disease, gall-stones, cholesterol problems and cancer.

Foods always contain some combination of fats, but usually one type predominates. The two main types of fats are satu-rated and unsaturated. Saturated fats are usually found in meats such as beef, pork and ham, and dairy products like whole milk, cream and cheese. Saturated fats are generally solid at room temperature.

Unsaturated fats are generally liquid at room temperature, and are not sticky like saturated fats. Most fish oils and vegetable oils are unsaturated. The two exceptions are coconut and palm oil. Don't be tricked by the clever marketing of some breakfast cereals for example—the coconut in many of them has the same effect on the body that other saturated fats do.

Regardless of the source, all fat has nine kilojoules per gram. However, not all fats are created equal—some have more nega-tive effects on our health than others—unsaturated fats are better for you then saturated fats. You can see this by looking at the diet of people living in the Mediterranean countries who eat a lot of olive oil, yet have low levels of heart disease and long life expectancy.

How to eliminate one pound of fat

While we are on the subject of fat, I thought you might find this interesting. There are 3,500 kilojoules in one pound (approximately 400 grams) of fat. To lose one pound of stored fat you need to eliminate 3,500 kilojoules. To do this you have two choices—you can cut 3,500 kilojoules from your food intake, or burn 3,500 more kilojoules than you eat, through exercising. Of course, you can always combine the kilojoule cutting with exercise—this is obviously the best option.

To give you an idea of what it takes to burn off 3,500 kilojoules (one pound of fat), take a look at these figures:

* you could walk for approximately 12 hours

* run for 3 hours

* cycle or swim for about 7 hours

* or better still, avoid eating the pound of fat in the first place.

There is indeed a lot to be said for an eating plan that is based mainly on fruit and vegetables.

Cholesterol

Cholesterol is a fatty substance found in animal products like beef, cheese, milk and eggs. Cholesterol and fat are not the same thing—unlike fat, cholesterol has no kilojoules. Small amounts are essential for hormones and brain and nerve cells. However, excess levels of cholesterol cause blocked arteries, especially leading to the heart and brain.

If you eat foods that are high in saturated fat, your body will produce more cholesterol. To reduce your level of cholesterol, reduce the amount of saturated fat in your diet, rather than eliminating the foods that contain cholesterol. It is also wise to lose any excess weight that you may be carrying. Have your doctor check your cholesterol level, particularly if your intake of saturated fats is high.

Fruit and vegetables

Seventy per cent of the planet is made up of water, and so too are our bodies. It makes sense then that we have an eating plan high in water-rich foods. The best sources of these foods are fruit and vegetables. An eating plan based on water-rich foods allows your body to cleanse itself, flushing out any nasty toxins. Not only do fruit and vegetables provide a good source of complex carbohydrates and water, they are also rich in vitamins and fibre. Vitamins A, C and E, found in fruit and vegetables, are important in protecting the body from disease.

Fibre

Fibre is found in plant foods like wholegrain cereals, grains, fruit, vegetables, dried fruit, legumes, seeds and nuts. Although dairy products and meat contain other essential nutrients, they contain absolutely no fibre. Neither do processed foods like cakes and chocolate. Fibre is essential in developing and maintaining a healthy body. However, there is very little fibre in the food most people consume today. Eating a wide range of plant foods will ensure that you get the full range of fibre your body needs.

There are many advantages in increasing the amount of fibre in your diet—it keeps you regular, it can prevent heart disease and colon cancer, and can help prevent haemorrhoids. You will also feel full after eating fibre because it is bulky, so you won't feel like eating for a while afterwards. The good news is foods that are high in fibre are usually low in fat.

Start the day off right

The word 'breakfast' was originally two words—'break' and 'fast'. Its meaning is simply to break the fast, or time without food, between dinner the night before and lunch the following day. Many people skip breakfast and eat their entire day's food at lunch and dinner, and then eat nothing until lunch the next day. This means that they deprive their body of food for approximately seventeen hours. And if they do have anything in the morning it is usually only a cup of coffee or two. Obviously, this is not the best way to start your day. You are not providing your body or mind with the fuel and energy it needs to get you through each morning, let alone perform at its optimum.

Don't be tempted to skip breakfast. The excuse of not having enough time or not feeling like it is again self defeating if your goal is to lose weight. Skipping breakfast actually lowers your metabolic rate and an important factor in losing weight is to increase your metabolism, not lower it.

A great way to start the day is to have a breakfast built on complex carbohydrates—foods like cereal, porridge, toast, fruit and freshly squeezed juice. This kind of breakfast will provide you with sustained energy to keep you going until lunchtime.

You may have trained yourself over the years not to want breakfast, so the best way of re-training your body is to start by having something small each morning, and build it up until breakfast becomes your main meal of the day. It may be a little difficult at first to break your old habits, but training your body to want and enjoy breakfast is essential in improving your overall health and fitness.

By skipping breakfast, hurrying lunch, and making dinner your main meal of the day, your body doesn't have much of a chance to use the energy it gets from the food you eat at night. As a result, most of the unused food is taken to bed with you and is stored as fat. It's a matter of reversing what you have probably been doing for years and instead aiming to eat breakfast like a king, lunch like a prince and dinner like a pauper.

Eating healthy foods not only increases your energy and makes you feel great, it also shows in your appearance. You'll find that people who follow a healthy eating program more often than not have clear skin, healthy hair, and an overall 'glow'.

Keep in mind that it's what you do consistently, not what you do occasionally that matters. So don't restrict your eating to exclude all of your favourite foods. By doing this, you'll eventually resent your attempts to improve your health and fitness, and revert back to a less than healthy eating plan. It isn't necessary to deprive yourself totally, but you will find that the healthier you become, the less you'll feel like the chocolates, biscuits and sweets.

Keep these figures in mind:

One gram of fat contains 37 kilojoules.
One gram of protein contains 17 kilojoules.
One gram of carbohydrate contains 16 kilojoules.
One gram of alcohol contains 29 kilojoules.

Don't believe the hype

Spot reduction

Although you may have heard that it is possible to lose weight from one particular area of your body, this is simply not true. This fallacy, known as spot-reduction, has had people tricked for years. When you lose weight you lose it from your entire body—from your arms, legs, buttocks, face—not just a certain area.

Fat-free does not mean kilojoule free

Many people believe that they can eat any amount of something if it is fat-free—again, this is false. You'll find that fat-free foods are usually high in kilojoules, as sugar is often substituted for the fats to make up for a loss of taste. If your body uses fewer kilojoules than you consume, those kilojoules will be stored as fat, regardless of their source.

A diet based on junk food

Another common myth is that it's OK to eat junk food, or negative foods, if you exercise. You can exercise all you like, but no amount of huffing and puffing will make up for an eating plan based on low quality foods. Junk food has few, if any, of the nutrients that are needed to keep your body strong and to fight off disease. Your body can only be as good as the food you put into it, and without the right dose of positive foods, your body is unable to perform at its peak.

Some points to keep in mind

* Try to avoid eating a large meal in the evening—eating at night doesn't give you a chance to burn off any of your food's kilojoules, and what your body hasn't burnt off, you take to bed with you. Also try to avoid snacking late at night.

* Remember to treat yourself. Being too strict with yourself can be de-motivating. Allow yourself to indulge every now and then. A good rule of thumb is to eat healthy foods ninety per cent of the time, and be less strict on yourself for the other ten. Another trick is to allow yourself one 'cheat day' per week. After getting into your exercise routine, you'll find that your taste buds will change and your craving for junk food will diminish.

* Don't rush your meals—allow your stomach a chance to feel full by pausing between each mouthful. It takes approximately twenty minutes for your mind to register that any food has reached your stomach.

* Don't eat when you are feeling stressed, anxious or excited—you are much more likely to rush your meal if you are not relaxed. It's also tougher to digest your food if you are stressed.

* Eat regularly, and don't skip meals—skipping meals actually slows your metabolism. Your body is tricked into thinking that the next meal is a long way off, so it holds onto its stores. You are also more likely to overeat when you are next around food simply because you are so hungry.

* Limit the amount of caffeine that you consume daily—coffee, tea, chocolate and cola all contain caffeine. It takes approximately twenty-four hours for just one cup of tea or coffee to pass through your kidneys and urinary tract.

* Be kind to your body—remember that what goes into your body must be either used or eliminated.

Excuses don't stack up

Improving your level of health and fitness will require a considerable amount of effort and commitment. It won't happen overnight, and it won't happen if you decide to do nothing about it. Make a decision to trash the old excuses—not having enough time or energy, not liking exercise or being too lazy. These excuses serve no purpose, other than to keep you unfit and unhealthy.

To get past these excuses, find an exercise that you enjoy, maybe grab a friend to train with, and start to experience and appreciate the benefits that come from a fit and healthy body and mind. Remember it only takes twenty-one days to form a new habit. Make today the first day.

Topic	Page
Assessing your fitness level	50
Your target heart rate	53
What are your goals?	57
The F.I.T.T. Principle	63
P.R.I.C.E.D.	69
What do we mean by metabolic rate or metabolism?	75
Positive and negative foods	78
Some points to keep in mind	87

Notes on Health and Fitness

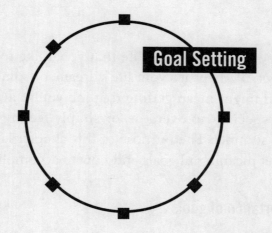

Goal Setting

Goals provide you with direction and focus:
they work like a road map, helping you
reach your destination.

Goal Setting

Is there something in your life that you'd like to achieve, but haven't yet? Perhaps it's your life's dream, or something a little smaller. It might mean getting that job you've always wanted, taking a special trip overseas, or simply feeling and looking great for summer. The purpose of this chapter is to show you how to set meaningful goals and how to accomplish them.

The importance of goals

The purpose of setting goals is to provide you with direction throughout your life. Goals are like a road map for you to follow in getting to your destination—they allow you to monitor your progress, and help you stay on the right track. Goals give you focus and purpose, and focusing your resources toward a particular set of goals is one of the most important steps in improving the quality of your life.

It may surprise you to know that most people never take the time to set a single major goal in their entire lifetime. In fact, of the entire world population less than three per cent of people have their goals written down, and of these three per cent less than one per cent actually refer to them on a regular basis. This means that a staggering ninety-seven of people are living with no clear plan of their goals at all, or any idea of how near or far they might be from achieving them. Ask yourself which group you belong to.

Success or failure—the choice is yours

Your level of success in life will be determined by your ability to set goals and then follow through in achieving them. It's a strong statement, but without goals, success and happiness will be almost impossible to achieve. If you want outstanding results from life you need to become proactive, never simply accepting what life serves you.

Accepting responsibility for where you are in life now is crucial. If you are happy with your life, congratulations. But if you find yourself regularly dissatisfied then it is time to do something about it. Success is about realising that you alone are responsible for what you have achieved to date. Until you accept the responsibility, your direction and purpose in life will remain unchanged. Setting goals is an important step in realising your potential. Understand that there is nothing to stop you from achieving your goals—whether or not you achieve your goals depends on how strong your desire is.

Move beyond your comfort zone

Our comfort zones are the boundaries that we live each day according to. We are comfortable with the things we do and the thoughts we have—they are not challenging or threatening, and there is no anxiety or fear of failure. We are secure in our activities and thoughts. For example, in building a career as a drummer, there has to be a stage where you go from practising in the safe and secure environment of your bed-room or garage, to playing your first gig in front of a live audience. Moving beyond a situation where you feel comfort-able to one where there is potential for embarrassment can be terrifying, but is not only necessary, it is also extremely rewarding and satisfying. And the hunger you develop to do it again is insatiable.

Many people are content to live day to day, and are satisfied if they make it through each day without a major hiccup. How-ever, it is these people that question why they are in the same situation now that they were in years before. It is easy to become stuck in a rut and to find excuses that explain why you haven't achieved. What many people fail to realise is that doing more of the same will only give them more of the same. You can't expect your life to change if you are not prepared to make the changes, starting within yourself.

Performing at your peak means taking a giant step outside your comfort zone. It also means accepting that change is a necessary key to moving you from where you are today to where you want to be. Being proactive is about setting specific goals, and this is something that most people simply fail to do.

Ask yourself what you really want from life. Where do you want to be in five, ten or even thirty years from now? Are your answers to these questions motivating and powerful, or boring and stale? Let's face it, setting a goal to make it to work on time, or simply to pay the bills when they're due, isn't really inspiring enough to make you jump out of bed each morning full of enthusiasm, is it? The goals you set for yourself must be aimed at improving the quality of your life—question how your goals contribute to your life. It's important not to think small, but rather to look at the big picture. Set the kind of goals that will inspire you each day. And above all, realise that life has given you what you've asked for so far. If you don't provide your life with direction and set out to achieve a specific outcome by knowing what you want, how will life know what it should give you?

How to set goals that produce results

Setting goals that produce the kind of results you want requires that you know where you are now and where you want to be in the future. What are the priorities in your life? What really matters to you? Take some time to consider what you want from life.

In deciding your goals for each area of life, you might find it helpful to use the 'S.M.A.R.T.' technique to goal setting. It's simple, effective and easy to remember.

Specific   You need to be clear about what you want to achieve. Be as specific as possible because the more you focus your efforts, the more powerful the outcome will be.

Measurable   Break your goal down into smaller pieces—that way you'll know that you're on track as you achieve each small goal. It's also very motivating to know that you are achieving along the way.

Attributable   Understand that you are personally responsible for achieving your goals. Don't play the role of the victim. Remember, you are at cause, and not effect.

Realistic   Your goals have to be possible to accomplish yet make you stretch beyond your comfort zone. Be careful not to set unrealistic goals, as these can be demotivating.

Time limit Set a realistic deadline for each goal—a definite date that you want to achieve your goals by. This forces you to focus your efforts and resources.

Once you've set your goals, you need to concentrate on achieving them. When it comes to deciding the goals that will improve the quality of your life, it's important that you include short-term goals that will give you direction along the way. Achieving your short-term goals will allow you to measure how you're going, and will also give you the motivation and confidence to keep at your longer-term goals.

Remember that what you truly believe and focus on you will move towards. You have to prepare your body and mind for success—condition them in an empowering and positive way. Train your brain by acting now the way you would if you had already achieved your goals. Feel them, see them, and hear them—your subconscious mind is subjective and doesn't know the difference between what is real and what is not. Provide your mind with positive references over and over again, and eventually your mind will believe that they are real. And what's more, they soon will be.

Planning pays

In achieving any goal, there are a number of options available to you. For example, your goal might be to lose ten kilos. Now to do this, you could look at taking the dog for a walk three times a week, or walking to and from work if it's not too far. Or if you are a little more energetic, you might consider joining a gym and taking an aerobics class every second day.

You need to decide on the best option—the one that will give you the results you want in the time you want. This means looking at the pros and cons of each option. For example, if you decide that walking is the answer, then the financial outlay is simply a matter of investing in a good pair of walking shoes and finding an interesting place to walk. However, if you decide to join the gym as a means of reaching your goal then you need to consider the financial cost of the membership and the motivation needed to get you there at least three times a week. And of course, time is another factor that you need to look at. Do you have the time to drive to and from the gym every second day, or is walking around the neighbourhood or to and from work more time-effective? Evaluating your options may take a while to do, but planning how you'll achieve each of your goals will take you one giant step closer to where you really want to be.

Persistence pays too

You need to focus and be dedicated to seeing your goals come to life. A word of warning—it won't happen overnight. You need to be persistent—any real change will require effort on your part. You must be dedicated to your constant improvement. A half-hearted effort will give you less than half-hearted results. Don't let the fear of failure stop you from achieving all you deserve in life. If you try something and it doesn't work then change tack. Keep trying until you find the way to reach every single one of your goals.

Thomas Edison, the inventor of the electric light bulb, is a great example of how persistence pays. He took the meaning of persistence and stretched it beyond all limitations. It took him more than 11,000 attempts before he successfully came up with the first working light bulb. And what did he say about each of the 11,000 attempts that didn't work? Just this—'I didn't fail 11,000 times, but I successfully found 11,000 ways that did not work'.

If your efforts don't show an immediate return then keep persisting, and don't give up too soon. More often than not, people that give up on their goals are so close to seeing them come to life, but quit just that little bit too early and fail to reach their full potential. You'll soon realise that before any great success can be achieved there will probably be a number of failures or lessons to be learned. It's what you learn from each experience that set's you apart.

Working backward to achieve your goals

It may seem like a strange way to go about achieving your goals, but working backward really does work. I use a simple and effective method known as the 'Pert' chart. The technique requires that you decide what end result you want from each of your goals and then work backwards step by step from that end result to now.

The astronauts used the very same technique to land on the moon. What do you think their desired end result might have been before they set off? Was it actually landing on the moon? No. What they really wanted was to make it back to earth safe and well. To achieve this they had to detail absolutely everything that needed to happen—from the original thought of first wanting to land on the moon right through to making it home safely after a successful mission. Let me explain how you can combine the Pert technique with modelling to achieve any of your goals.

If your goal is to become the top sprinter at the local athletics club by the beginning of the next season, you might start by finding someone who has already achieved an outstanding level of success in the same field and copy or model their success. Successful people are the key to producing the results you want. You'll need to examine closely everything about them that has led to their success. This includes both their physiology and psychology.

Study their nutritional habits; what training equipment they use and what clothing they wear; how often they train and the length of each training session; how they relax; how they walk and how they talk. Just as importantly, look at their mental attitude, the way they approach each challenge. In fact, learn as much as possible about the person you intend to model. Each piece of information you collect then becomes a mini-goal that you must then adapt to suit yourself and incorporate into your life—this will set you on the right course for achieving the result you're aiming for.

Once you are satisfied with how much information you've collected, you can then apply the Pert method. You now know how to achieve the end result you're after, so the next step is to work backwards from this end result, by deciding on a schedule to achieve each of the smaller goals. How hard you have to work to achieve your goal will depend on how much time you have up your sleeve. For example, if you have recognised six vital areas you need to perfect to achieve your goal, and you have a six month time limit, your aim then is to perfect one area per month until all you have all six areas down pat.

You'll recognise the improvements in yourself with each smaller goal you accomplish, and by the end of this process you should be experiencing the kind of results you have always dreamed of.

Create the momentum to move you

It's crucial that you do something every day that moves you toward achieving each of your goals. Whether you take a small or large step in the right direction is not the most important consideration—what's important is that you develop enough momentum to keep on keeping on. Look at your goals morning and night, and live as though they are already a part of your life. The more momentum you create, the faster you will succeed. You'll also find that your energy levels will reach an all time high, and your motivation to succeed will be a burning desire.

My Ultimate Goal

I am committed to

over the next   weeks/months.

To achieve my ultimate goal I have identified the following areas that will become my mini-goals   **Deadline**

Notes on Goal Setting

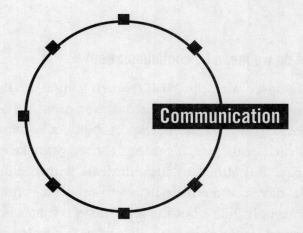

Communication

Learn how to speak the language of others to develop trust and rapport in every situation.

Communication

What do we mean by communication?

If you agree with the NLP (Neuro Linguistic Programming) definition, the meaning of communication is simply the response you elicit. If the responsibility of communication lies with each of us then it's essential that we make every effort to improve our ability to communicate with the people around us. It may sound a little heavy to say that communication is your responsibility, but the good news is that it isn't difficult to be a great communicator—all it takes is a little practise.

A good place to start is by explaining that each of us perceives the world differently. What is interesting is that we don't perceive reality—we perceive our own model of reality. We perceive the world through our senses—we take in information through our sight, touch, taste, hearing and sense of smell, and how we take in this information forms our very own model of the world. In other words, every person has a different model or way of perceiving the world.

Now, if every person's model is unique then the issue of communication is even more important than you might think. We can't assume that because we come from the same area, or speak the same language, or have the same interests that effective communication will naturally happen—it just isn't the case. There are some subtleties that we need to consider.

The power of Neuro Linguistic Programming

Neuro Linguistic Programming (NLP) is a very powerful therapy that can help improve your communication skills by bridging any gaps in the way you communicate. NLP looks at the different ways we think and communicate with each other, both verbally and non-verbally. I'm sure you've had times when you simply couldn't relate to others, and no matter what you said or did you simply couldn't get your point across. We'll look at some of the reasons why communication can be difficult and also how to overcome these difficulties.

The 'instant connection'

I'm sure you've been in a situation where you felt an almost instant connection with someone, even if you had never met them before. It may be that you were sitting the same way, or using the same words, or even making the same gestures. Whatever the case, you just seemed to hit it off with this person for no particular reason. You probably weren't consciously aware of what was happening, but the connection was something you couldn't ignore. The reason for this connection is what we call rapport. You see, when two people are alike it is easier for them to like each other.

The magic of rapport

Trust is essential for effective communication, and the backbone of trust is rapport. People will automatically move towards those that they trust. In fact, without rapport success-ful communication is almost impossible. If you want the right response from your communication then it's a good idea to practise building rapport with others. This ability is one of the most important skills you can have. In short, trust = rapport = effective communication.

Building rapport shows the other person that you understand their model of the world. This is important because each of us believes that our individual model of the world is real. Rapport is a great way to build a strong bond between yourself and the other person. By making a genuine effort to consider someone else's model of the world you'll find that communication will be easier, more effective and much more enjoyable.

How to create rapport

The most effective way of creating rapport is by matching the other person, and you can acknowledge their model of the world by matching their language, or by matching their physiology.

Using language to create rapport

To match someone's model of the world through language, it's important to understand that we can experience the world through what we see, smell, hear, feel and taste. At any given moment we are using all of our senses to receive and process information. However, when it comes to developing our own model of the world, we tend to rely primarily on one of our senses—this reliance is known as our representational system.

There are three basic methods, or representational systems, that people use to perceive the world around them. These are *auditory*, *visual* and *kinesthetic*. People who are auditory hear their world, visuals see their world, and kinesthetics feel it. Our representational systems help us to relate to the world and understand it. What's interesting is that we don't consciously choose to use one representational system over another—it happens on an unconscious level.

Although we tend to be auditory, visual or kinesthetic, we don't rely on one system to the exclusion of the others. We are constantly taking in information through our senses, and our minds switch from one system to another. In improving your communication skills, it is important to realise that each of us has a preferred way of interpreting the world that we are most comfortable with.

Determining someone's representational system

You'll notice that during a conversation the other person will use consistent words and phrases, and it is the use of these words and phrases that will show you the representational system through which they experience the world. Determining someone's primary representational system, and then speaking to them in their 'language' makes developing rapport easy. Can you pick the representational system in each of these examples?

'Have you ever seen anything so beautiful? I just love the view from here at this time of day. Look at the colours in the sunset—amazing reds, oranges and pinks. I could sit here and look out for hours.'

Now consider how someone else might experience the same situation.

'Listen to the waves lapping the beach—they sound so calm. It's as if they have a voice of their own. Their timing is so perfect. If you listen carefully you can hear the echo in the caves down below.'

Again, the same situation, but from a different representational system.

'I feel so relaxed and comfortable sitting here. I haven't felt this relaxed for a long time. It reminds me of the holidays I spent with my best friend—we hadn't been in touch for years. We spent the time laughing and remembering how it felt to be young. Those memories are worth holding onto.'

You probably picked the first example as visual. The use of 'seen', 'view', 'colours—amazing reds, oranges and pinks', and 'look out' pinpoint which representational system this person relies upon. Because this person's description of the world is so visual, they are able to create a picture of a situation so vividly that we are able to 'see' in our mind the situation they are describing.

Visuals use words such as 'see', 'look', 'focus', 'watch', 'show', 'bright', 'picture', 'illustrate' and 'clear' throughout a conversation. The phrases they use include 'Looks good to me', 'I can picture that', 'Can you show me?', 'It's clear to me', and so on.

The second example is auditory. Again, the use of certain words like 'listen', 'lapping', 'sound', 'voice', 'rhythm' and 'hear' make it easy to understand and enter this person's model of the world. Other words that auditories use include tone, say, and speak. Auditories will use phrases like 'That rings a bell', 'That sounds great', 'Did you hear what happened last week?' 'Can you tell me how this works?'

And the third example is kinesthetic. Kinesthetic people are very much in tune with their emotions and feelings. They'll use words and phrases such as 'relaxed', 'feel', 'comfortable', 'in touch', and 'holding onto' to describe their world and how they perceive it. You'll often hear a kinesthetic person using phrases such as 'He rubs me the wrong way', 'That just doesn't feel right', 'I've got a handle on the situation', 'Let's touch base next week' and 'Let's grab some lunch'.

What is interesting with each of these examples is that the situation is given—a beach scene at sunset—but how each of the three people describes and experiences the situation is so different. After a while you'll begin to recognise that each system has its own language. It may not always be obvious straight away, but determining the other person's representational system will become much easier simply by paying attention to the words and phrases they use frequently.

Recognising these systems and then speaking to a person using their own language is a great way to build the strong sense of rapport essential to effective communication. There is no need for the other person to translate what you are saying into their own language—you've already done it. The result is that the other person will feel more comfortable being with you and will be much more trusting of you. Miscommunication is also less likely to happen because you are both speaking the same 'language'. Using the appropriate words and phrases shows that you understand what the other person is experiencing. This will give you an advantage when it comes to developing meaningful relationships. Let me show you how powerful this information can be.

I want you to imagine for a minute that you are a car salesperson. Now unfortunately the reputation of this profession has not been too positive to date. I must admit that when I've bought cars in the past I was usually on the defence before entering the car yard. So rather than working from a level playing field the salesperson had to do some pretty fancy talking just to win me back to neutral territory.

Now remember that rapport is essential in developing trust between two people, and without a strong sense of rapport it is unlikely that a sale will take place. So here's how a salesperson could approach a sale the next time he is talking to a visual:

'Jim, isn't the colour great. Can't you just picture yourself driving this new model Mercedes? You look great in it. The interior has been especially colour co-ordinated to match the trim of the vehicle. Can you see how the body has been designed to look sleek and elegant? How does the total package look to you?'

By using this language the customer is able to see what the salesperson is describing. Simply by pointing out the visual aspects of the product and using visually based words and phrases, the level of rapport and trust automatically increases.

Now, if the salesperson were selling the same vehicle to an auditory, it would simply be a matter of changing a few words and phrases used throughout the conversation. Rather than stressing the visual qualities of the vehicle, the salesperson would place importance on the auditory qualities. For example, they would point out how smooth the engine sounds, or the quality of the sound system installed. The salesperson might also have the customer honk the horn, or test the radio—anything to do with the auditory aspects of the vehicle. It might sound a little strange, but it can mean the difference between developing the rapport that's needed to clinch the sale, and losing the customer through poor communication.

When selling to a kinesthetic, the salesperson might have the customer sit in the vehicle to 'get a feel for the car'. Or ask them to adjust the mirrors and the seat to make it as comfortable as possible. Have them play with the radio, change the gears, point out the safety features and how reliable the vehicle is, and anything else that 'might grab them'. Ask them 'how much they would feel comfortable spending', or 'if there is enough leg room for them to sit comfortably'. They'll soon tell you how they feel towards the vehicle and you'll get the feedback you want simply by asking the right questions.

Using physiology to create rapport

The verbal cues we have just discussed are the easiest to recognise and use in developing rapport, but there are a number of other cues that you can use to determine someone's representational system.

The characteristics and traits of a visual

Visuals make sense of the world by turning everything that is said to them into pictures. In other words, they think by making pictures in their mind. A visual person will make sense of what you are saying by comparing your words to the pictures in their mind that they associate with each word.

As you might expect, a visual will be most concerned with the visual aspects of a situation. When they interact with other people they take particular notice of facial expressions, dress, gestures and other movements. Their first impressions of a situation or person are often based on appearance. In fact, if something is visually incorrect it can throw a visual person right off track. For example, something as simple as a salesperson with a crooked necktie or dirty hands can distract a visual to the point of the salesperson losing the sale. Needless to say, appearance is important for visuals.

Remembering and describing how things looked in great detail is simple for a visual—ask a visual to tell you about their third grade teacher, and notice how they are able to paint a picture of the teacher for you. Visuals have great memories when it comes to shapes, colours and sizes.

Visuals will often stand back from a situation to get the best overall view and will position themselves so they can see the other person or the situation as clearly as possible. Visuals must be able to see to understand what is going on. They like to interpret information by actually looking at it.

During a conversation, a visual may interrupt you to make sure that you understand what they have to say. You'll notice that they speak quickly and that their voices are usually high pitched. Their posture is also straight, and their breathing is from high in their chest.

To improve how you communicate with visuals, talk to them in their language—use words and phrases that are visually based. Using analogies or examples will go a long way in communicating effectively with visuals. Their response will be positive. They'll easily understand what you want to communicate, and developing a level of rapport will happen almost immediately.

The characteristics and traits of an auditory

Auditories will listen to what is going on around them and make sense of their world through sound. They place a lot of emphasis not only on what is said, but also on how it is said. In fact they tend to get most of their information from the way something is said—intonation, tone, pace and timbre—all are extremely important to someone who is auditory.

Auditories are perhaps more familiar with 'foot in the mouth' than visuals or kinesthetics. To understand what they are thinking they need to actually hear their words, and so they tend to think out loud. Of course, once something has been said it's difficult to take it back.

Auditories will often speak to themselves or mumble. They find it useful to talk their problems through out loud, even if it is only with themselves. They respond to sounds, particularly the sound of their own voice. For this reason, sounding good is important. When they speak they are conscious of every word that leaves their mouth. Their voice is rhythmical, steady and clear, and their breathing is somewhat slow and deep.

Auditories avoid eye contact. They tend to look away from the person they are speaking to, and feel uncomfortable if they are forced to make eye contact. They also find it easier to concentrate if their attention isn't being distracted by having to make eye contact. Being able to see or touch the person they are speaking to is not important, but being in a position to hear clearly what they are saying is.

The characteristics and traits of a kinesthetic

Rather than interpret the world through what they see or hear, kinesthetics actually feel what goes on around them. They use their emotions, touch and gut instinct to guide their actions. Kinesthetics place a great deal of importance on feelings in order to make sense of what is happening.

First impressions are important—kinesthetics will decide almost immediately whether or not they like someone based on their feelings toward that person. They like to be close enough to actually touch the person they are speaking to, and this close proximity is how they gain the information they need to understand a situation. Kinesthetics would rather touch than look, so maintaining eye contact isn't important.

During a conversation, often without thinking, they'll pick up an object to play with. The object might be a pen, a piece of paper, or even something they are wearing. This 'fiddling' makes them feel comfortable and at home in the situation. To emphasise their point in a conversation they'll touch the person they are speaking with, usually on the arm, the back, or the shoulder—this kind of interaction is important in developing rapport with a kinesthetic.

Because kinesthetics think with their feelings it takes them longer to access the information they need. As a result, they'll often pause in a conversation. Don't butt in during their pauses—it's important that you give them the time they need to access their emotions and to think about the situation. A kinesthetic's voice is usually slow and soft, so slowing your speech and the way you deliver your information will add to the rapport they feel with you.

Determining your representational system

We all have a favoured representational system we rely on when we communicate, whether it be visual, auditory or kinesthetic. In developing outstanding communication skills it is not enough to simply determine the other person's representational system—you also need to understand where your own thoughts are coming from. You'll find it almost impossible to improve your level of rapport with someone if you haven't established which representational system you operate from.

Start by spending one minute thinking about your last holiday. You can do this with a friend, or by yourself. Take notice of the words you use to describe the holiday and write them down. At the end of the minute look at your list—how did you describe your holiday? What was most important—what you saw? What you heard? Or what you felt? You'll probably notice that the words you use favour one representational system. In fact, it might have been difficult to remember anything about your holiday in the other representational systems.

We all have different ways of interpreting the world around us, and we are more comfortable putting our trust in those people that perceive the world the way we do. Communicating with someone in their own style will enable you to develop rapport faster and more effectively because you are showing that you understand the other person and their view of the world. They will be interested in what you have to say, and will also feel that what they have to say is important.

Notes on Communication

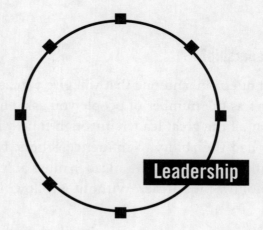

Leadership

Your level of success in life is directly related to
your ability to influence others in a positive way.

Leadership

What is leadership?

It's a good question, and one that will give you as many different answers as the number of people you ask. However, when you look at all the great leaders through time, you'll find that they each had the ability to influence others. I know that it sounds rather simplistic, but a leader must able to influence others to follow him or her. Without a following there is no leader.

Why everyone should learn to lead

It's not just the supervisor at work or the captain on the local football team who needs to be a great leader. If you agree that leadership is the ability to influence people then you'll also agree that anyone who has contact with other people should learn how to lead.

You may be questioning whether you really need to develop your skills as a leader. If this is the case then you'll find it interesting to know that even shy and reserved people will influence thousands of people during their lifetime. Keep in mind that influencing someone may be as simple as recommending a certain car to your younger sister, a great local restaurant to the new neighbours, or in a work situation you might recommend one brand over another to a customer. These are all examples of how we influence people each day. This means that every one of us is both influencing and being influenced every day of our lives. Ask yourself how you are influencing others now. Are you leading in a way that will produce the results you want?

Leadership is a skill you can learn

I realise it's a strong statement, but the quality of your leadership skills will determine the level of your success. Why? Simply because your success is directly related to your ability to influence and lead others. Achieving any real level of success requires not only the support, but also the cooperation of other people. The ability to influence people is essential to your success as a leader. The good news is that not all great leaders were born great leaders—leadership is a quality and an ability that can be developed over time through experience. You can learn to become a great leader if you truly desire to.

Leadership—by consent or force?

There are basically two ways that a person can lead. The first is by consent. The second is by force. People who lead by force don't last long. Their leadership style may work in the short-term—people might fake their support, but even the faking is short-lived. Successful leaders understand that the support and cooperation of the people around them is vital, and that the better they treat others, the better others will respond to them. Successful leaders lead others in a humane way.

Lead by example

Leading others is a position of high responsibility—the people you're leading will pattern or model your thoughts and actions. They'll adjust what they expect from themselves based on the standards that you set for yourself. For this reason, you need to show total integrity and consistency. Make sure that you are worth modelling—there is no use in providing others with a lousy example of a leader. Be the person that you want others to be, and lead by example—you need to behave and think the way you want others to behave and think.

A shared vision

To lead others effectively you have to develop a shared vision. You have to develop common goals and dreams that each person can relate to so they will they want to participate. People will want to support you and do their best in a situation in which they have had input. Make sure that each person is a part of setting the goals, and watch their motivation shoot through the roof. You'll find that people will be more motivated when they are involved in setting directions and objectives because they know what is expected of them.

Understand that motivating people with money or by fear alone will have very limited advantages, if any—a shared vision and sense of purpose will do much more. If people are motivated by fear or by money they will only participate for as long as the fear and money are present.

The secret behind motivation

The desire to feel important is a strong motivational tool, and it is up to you as a leader to make others feel that way. Show that you really care and respect and trust the people around you and you will be surrounded by motivated people wanting to share in your vision.

You can't force people into succeeding. They will only excel if they decide to do so. They will only share in your dreams and aspirations if they feel important. In fact, seven of the most powerful words you can say to someone are 'What you do makes a real difference'. You need to treat people with respect and dignity, and reward them when they have done something they can be proud of.

The first concept in motivating someone, according to Dale Carnegie, is to include people. This means asking for and listening to the suggestions that are put forward, and working within a team environment where each person feels that they are making an important contribution. The second concept is to treat people as people—this means being interested in others, and acknowledging their importance. The third concept is to acknowledge a job well done. This means taking notice of what other people are doing well and congratulating them on it. After all, we all like to be told that we've done a good job.

Walk a mile in the other person's shoes

You must have a sense of empathy—you must be able to understand how others feel and appreciate each situation from the other person's point of view. Consider how things would look and feel and sound if you were the other person. Ask yourself 'How would I think/feel/respond if I was in this person's shoes?' You'll find that this will give you a much clearer picture of any situation you find yourself in.

Each of us has a different way of looking at the world that has been determined by our education, our income, and our general background, and as a successful leader it pays to remember this.

Show people that you are genuinely interested in them

Let's face it, we all love to be flattered, to feel important and special. If you want others to support you then start by expressing a genuine interest in them. Too often we get caught up in our own world and fail to notice that anyone else exists. If this sounds familiar then it may be a good time to start looking outside yourself. People will respond to your interest in them almost immediately. Showing a genuine interest in others will not only make them feel important, but you'll also find that you'll be less concerned with your own problems.

Expressing interest in someone can be as simple as smiling, saying hello, learning their name, remembering their birthday, asking how their day is going, or giving a genuine compliment when it's deserved. It's elementary, but it is amazingly effective in developing rapport.

The importance of recognition

Have you ever done something that you were extremely proud of, yet no one seemed to notice? How did you feel? Disheartened? Unimportant? Demotivated? And if this happened again and again what kind of an effort do you think you'd be prepared to put in? I'm sure you wouldn't give your best if no one seemed to care how hard you were trying.

Many people in a leadership position fail to realise just how powerful small acknowledgements can be. People love to be told that they're doing a great job, or that their efforts really make a difference. Encouragement and recognition will bring out the best in the people around you. In fact, recognising the effort someone has made can motivate them to the next level—from doing a great job, to one that is outstanding. And again, recognition doesn't have to be limited to financial rewards. It can be as simple as saying thank you, or sending a short note, or praising an employee in front of their peers. If you have appreciated the effort someone has made then make a point of telling them—the response will be amazing.

Dealing with criticism

Being a leader carries with it the responsibility of ensuring that the desired results are achieved. If someone isn't performing as they should, then it's up to you to fix it. So the issue isn't whether you fix the situation, but how you go about fixing it.

We all make mistakes, and while we may be comfortable pointing them out in other people, we're not too comfortable with others pointing out our own. It's important to remember that people don't like feeling embarrassed or put down. The process of criticism, even constructive criticism, is something that you should consider carefully. Criticism can destroy a person's self-esteem and their self-confidence. This simple four-step approach works well in overcoming and preventing difficulties on both sides:

Talk about the situation in private with the person involved. Never criticise in public—it's a sure way to turn people against you. Compliment the person. Point out their positives—praise them for what they are doing right and let them know that they are making a positive and meaningful contribution. Show exactly where the improvement is needed, and offer your help

if it is needed. End the discussion on a positive note by complimenting them again on something they do well. People will
respond better if you focus on what they do right, rather than
just on the things they do wrong.

Admitting your own mistakes will also help to develop a trusting relationship. If people can see that you are big enough to
admit your own mistakes then they'll appreciate your advice
and listen to you when you have feedback for them. Showing
that mistakes are not a cause for punishment will also encour-
age people to take risks and try new things. When people feel
comfortable, their creativity and performance improve dramatically. If making a mistake results in criticism, people are less
motivated to give it their all and put forward innovative and
new thoughts.

All too often we find ourselves wanting to criticise what the
people around us do, but you need to keep in mind that criticism will always find its way back to you. Putting someone else
down can sometimes make you feel better about yourself, but
anyone is capable of criticising. As a leader, the challenge is to
make yourself stand apart by showing genuine understanding
and compassion for others.

The importance of communication

The ability to communicate effectively is a real skill. Having
the ability to both talk and listen to others is unfortunately not
that common. However, these are skills you need to master if
you want to achieve any real level of success in leading people.
Communication must be one of your top priorities. Regardless
of how good your ideas are, if you can't communicate and
share them with others, they are worthless. To successfully
communicate with others you need to be approachable. Don't

close yourself off. Effective communication is a two-way process. Allow others to communicate freely with you.

Developing an environment that is conducive to open communication is absolutely essential. People will not listen to what you have to say, or say what they think, unless a strong sense of trust has been established. Developing the right kind of environment will not happen overnight. You have to show by your actions that you genuinely care and that you mean exactly what you say. Your actions must reflect your words. Not being true to your word will destroy any possibility of building a trusting relationship between yourself and others.

Make a real effort to understand how others feel by listening to their ideas and thoughts and anything that they have to contribute. Once they have shown trust in you by communicating openly don't turn around and criticise what they have shared. Remember, criticism is a sure way to undermine trust and to turn others against you.

Listening to others

Listening is so much more than just hearing what someone has to say. Listening requires that you give the other person your undivided attention. Again, people will respond almost immediately when you listen to them. Listening is also a great way to learn—it is impossible for you to know everything, so be open to what other people have to say and you might be surprised at just how much you can learn from them. Listening will also show you exactly where the other person's thoughts and feelings are coming from, and when you listen at this level, you'll be in a much stronger position to put your point across.

Remember each of us has one mouth and two ears, and we need to learn to use them in that proportion.

Developing others

An outstanding leader is not threatened by other people. In fact, it's just the opposite: a great leader makes it a priority to surround him or herself with outstanding people. The successful leader understands how important it is to develop the skills and abilities of others. This is what being a leader really means.

Encouraging others to grow will bring out the best in them. When people are encouraged to develop they will learn new skills, and with their new skills they will gain the confidence to try new things. When an individual has personally grown as a result of your support and guidance, you'll also find that their loyalty will increase dramatically.

Make a point of asking how you can help to develop the people around you. What kind of training, books, or courses are they interested in? Would they benefit by spending some time with someone who has been successful in the same field? Could this person act as a mentor? Take the time to find out what interests and inspires the people around you.

Practise discipline and set priorities

The ability to stay focused and disciplined is extremely important in becoming a great leader. Setting goals and deciding what you want to achieve is the most effective way of staying focused and concentrating your efforts.

Developing your knowledge and skill as a leader is a long-distance race, not a sprint. You have to be in it for the long term, and having clearly defined objectives will help you ignore those little distractions along the way that can take up a whole lot of time if you let them—it means deciding what is important to you, and knowing what to overlook. Decide what you have to do and what you can pass onto someone else to do. However, remember that as a leader, the final responsibility for any situation is something that you can never give up—you have to accept full responsibility for the actions others take, both good and bad.

Your priorities will become clearer the more organised you are. Also, with organisation comes the ability to plan and to follow through with your plans. If others around you can see this, they will be willing to cooperate with you and place their trust in you. Your priorities will continually change, and you'll need to reassess their importance and make the necessary changes to your schedule. The chapter on Time Management offers you some helpful advice on how to prioritise your day and stay on top of things.

Developing a positive mental attitude

You have the ability to make of a situation what you want, because life is ten per cent what happens to you and ninety per cent how you react. I mentioned earlier that leadership is a position of high responsibility because people will model your thoughts and actions, whether they are positive or negative. So if your thoughts and actions are negative it will be impossible to inspire others to success. It is your responsibility as a leader to create an environment that is positive and empowering, and the best place to start is with the thoughts in your head.

If your attitude is upbeat, others will be attracted to you and will want to be part of your success. Your enthusiasm for a situation will affect how others look at the same situation. Being excited yourself is the best way to get others excited and involved. Remember your mental attitude towards every situation will determine your outcome. You are what you think, and your attitude will rub off on those around you.

> If you'd like to know how to create a positive mental focus and change your self-limiting beliefs, take some time to read the Attitude section starting on page 15.

The importance of integrity—the mark of a true leader

If you are to develop a relationship with others based on trust, then a strong sense of integrity is essential. A leader operating with integrity understands that what a leader says and what a leader does must be one and the same. There can be no discrepancy between the two. Trust and integrity go hand in hand.

What you say and what you do must be the same if you want consistent results. For example, if you ask others to be at work on time, and you arrive on time, then so will they. However, if you arrive late after asking everyone else to arrive on time, the results will be inconsistent—some will arrive on time, while others will arrive late. People need to know that what you say, think and do will be consistent in every situation. They need to know they can rely on you. A lack of integrity on your part will undermine the trust or support others have placed in you.

We are all familiar with people that change to fit the situation they find themselves in—they might change how they speak, how they dress, or how they treat others. These people are chameleons. You never quite know what to expect from them, and as a result find it difficult to place your confidence in them. You must mean what you say, and you must be consistent. The more credible you are the more confidence others will place in you. Make sure that there is no difference between the person others think you are and the person you really are.

Notes on Leadership

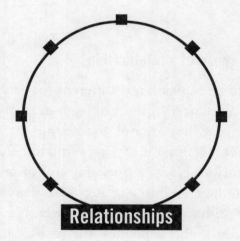

Relationships

Develop *the* ultimate friendship with
your partner and experience the magic of
a rewarding, satisfying relationship.

Relationships

What is the purpose of a relationship?

The answer to this question is different for each of us. Some people enter a relationship out of fear—fear of being left on the shelf, fear that they are not good enough, or fear that no one else will come along. Entering a relationship with these sorts of insecurities places a huge amount of pressure on the relationship. Others go into a relationship searching for companionship, intimacy, and love. However, the outcome for many can be quite the opposite—the result can be anything from pain and rejection through to despair and loneliness.

Sadly, a rewarding and successful relationship is something that many people fail to achieve. This is reflected in the high number of unsuccessful relationships that seem to be part of everyday life. For this trend to change, individuals need to change. For a relationship to be successful both people must have an understanding of how to make the relationship work and a commitment to seeing their relationship succeed.

Entering a relationship with the purpose of developing the ultimate friendship will allow you to experience the magic of a rewarding, satisfying relationship. The special feeling of fulfillment is something that can only come from a relationship based on trust and friendship. There is nothing quite as special as finding your soul mate—that one person you feel completely comfortable with, the one who inspires you, the one you can grow with and experience life with.

However, being in a relationship may not always be smooth sailing. What I'd like to offer you are some tips that I hope will allow you to experience the ultimate reward of a relationship— the pure happiness and bliss that it can bring.

Deciding who you are and what you want from a relationship

Before entering a relationship, it is important you have a good understanding of yourself and what you want to achieve from being in a relationship. You must be completely honest with yourself and address the issues that are important to you.

It makes little sense to dive into a relationship without first determining who you are. Despite this, few people know a great deal about themselves, about what makes them tick. Ask yourself what beliefs and values are most important to you. If this leaves you feeling a little puzzled then take some time now and in the coming weeks to decide how you feel about such issues as commitment, honesty, love, trust, marriage, children, fidelity, money and religion.

Your beliefs and values are the foundation of your personality, and I can't emphasise enough how important it is that you take some time to determine where you are really coming from. Once you have done this you'll be in a much better position to decide what kind of person you'd like as your partner.

The importance of goal setting in your relationship

Each of us has different needs and wants, and for us to feel complete, a unique blend of emotional, physical and spiritual needs must be met. Entering into a relationship shouldn't mean dismissing your individuality—in fact, your ability to achieve your needs should be enhanced. Just as you have particular needs and wants, so too does your partner. However, we tend to assume that our partner's needs and wants are the same as our own. We must recognise that we each have particular requirements, and for the relationship to be successful you must work towards satisfying your own needs and wants and those of your partner.

Working together to build the kind of relationship that completely fulfils both you and your partner will give you a level of satisfaction that is impossible to find elsewhere. It's too easy to give up and walk away when you come across a problem in your relationship. And chances are, your next relationship will be pretty similar if you enter it with the same attitude, skill and knowledge. The challenge is to use the information you have acquired to work at restoring and improving your relationship. Better still, if you can use this information as a way of preventing unhappiness in your relationship, then fantastic.

It is amazing the number of people who set financial, career or social goals, yet fail to recognise the importance of goal setting in their relationship. All too often, couples set out on building a life together, but fail to talk about what they really want from their relationship.

Developing a satisfying and rewarding relationship is about working towards a common set of goals with your partner. The goals will be different for each couple, but ultimately they

Relationships

should include all that you want from the relationship, both on an individual level and as a partnership.

The importance of taking the time to develop common goals with your partner is essential. To develop a meaningful long-term relationship your partner's beliefs and values must be compatible with your own. Talk about—the number of children you'd like to have and when; your commitment to marriage; your views on how work and marriage combine; your plans for travel and recreation; where and when you'd like to buy your own home—these issues should be addressed, not left to chance. Look at each issue that you hold close to your heart and determine exactly how your partner feels about it—make sure you have a clear understanding of what you both want from the relationship.

This doesn't mean that you'll agree on everything, and of course that's fine. What's important is that you have an understanding of each other's beliefs and values and that you respect where your partner is coming from. This will then enable you to develop realistic goals for your relationship together. Assuming that your partner wants the same things from the relationship that you do can be your undoing. Be at cause, not effect—communicate what you both want and then work towards those goals.

How we express love

The reason most relationships fail is the inability of both partners to communicate effectively. Ineffective communication is the cause of most problems. It's not a question of whether communication is taking place—the question is how effective and purposeful the communication is. Because we understand our own needs and how we like to be loved, we assume that our partner has the same understanding. This is rarely the case. It is important to recognise that you have your own needs, and it is up to you to develop the skills to communicate them. After all, communication is only effective when your message has been properly received by your partner.

As you can imagine, there is quite a lot of room for error and poor judgement when it comes to communication. The skill of effective communication is not something that we are taught. At best, we learn how to communicate by modelling those around us, like our parents and friends. The problem is that more often than not, our parents and friends are not always effective communicators themselves. Although it takes two to make a relationship work—or fail—you must take responsibility for your role in the communication that takes place. Don't allow your efforts to be hit and miss. Developing your skills and knowledge of communication may be something of a challenge, but it will be a most rewarding one.

Set aside some time to read the chapter on Communication. It explains that there are three basic methods, or representational systems, that we use to perceive the world around us. The methods are auditory, visual and kinesthetic. How you communicate and relate to others depends on your representational system.

Relationships can be a cause of frustration and concern. There are a number of theories that describe the innate differences between men and women. However, rather than offer explanations based on gender, I'd like to offer a different perspective. It is based on the teachings of NLP (Neuro Linguistic Programming). NLP looks at the way we communicate—it is a term for describing the psychology behind communication. It doesn't base our communication differences on gender, but rather on the way we experience the world around us.

As we talked about in the chapter on communication, different people have different ways of experiencing the world; auditory people 'hear' their world, visuals 'see' it, and kinesthetics 'feel' it. Understanding how others experience the world is a key factor in any relationship.

I want you to think back to a time when you had just fallen in love with someone special. You probably made every effort to make that person feel great, and nothing was too much trouble. Falling in love is one stage in our lives when our major representational system isn't ruling how we experience the world. You see, in our desire to make the other person feel special and to communicate how we feel, we make use of all our senses. There is rarely a problem in the early stages of a relationship, but once the 'honeymoon' period is over, both people fall back into their preferred way of experiencing the world and this is where the communication problems can begin.

Let me give you an example. Let's say that you are auditory and your partner is kinesthetic. His way of expressing love is through touch—maybe brushing your hair or massaging your back, but what you really want is for him to tell you that he loves you. Your way of expressing love is to compliment your partner. You might tell him what a wonderful job he has done, or how proud you are, yet all he wants is for you to touch him—he's after the physical reassurance that you care and that you are proud.

You can see that to be effective in a relationship it is important that both people learn to communicate with each other. This means learning, understanding and communicating in your partner's language. This is especially important if their language is different from your own.

Maybe you have heard your partner say, 'He doesn't show me that he loves me', or 'He never tells me that he loves me', or, 'I don't feel that he loves me'. Believe it or not, these sentences alone give you a strong indication as to your partner's representational system. Let me show you how this is relevant.

For those who are auditory

If your partner is auditory, verbal compliments and appreciation are essential. Tell your partner how much they mean to you, or how great it is being in their company. The full extent of your love will not be realised by rubbing their back or massaging their scalp—it will not mean as much to your auditory partner as telling them how special and important they are. The secret here is to tell, tell, tell, and tell it loud. Compliment your partner each time they do something good. Tell them how much you appreciate everything they do. You'll also find that by complimenting your partner using the language they understand, they are far more likely to return the compliment. Tell your partner exactly what you love about them and watch them grow into a person you can truly respect and admire.

Don't demand things from your auditory partner—learn to ask for or request things from them. Telling, or lecturing, only builds feelings of resentment, and your partner will refuse to listen or accept what you have to say. Requesting means that they have a choice whether or not to do what you ask. Also develop the habit of saying positive, uplifting things about your partner, both when you're together, and also when they're not around.

For those who are visual

Visual people experience their world through what they see, and what better way to please your visual partner then to give them a special gift that they can remember for years to come. The actual gift itself doesn't have to be expensive. The gift is not the most important thing—what matters is that you are expressing your love in the language that your partner understands. Giving a gift is simply a way of making your love tangible.

Telling your visual partner that you love them is nice, but their response will be much greater when you show them how you feel. By giving your visual partner a gift they have a symbol of your love that they can actually see.

You can also express love for your visual partner by doing small things for them that show you care. It might be running them a bath, or making a cup of tea at the end of a long day. What's important is that your visual partner can see that you are doing something special for them.

For those who are kinesthetic

The most effective and direct way to communicate with a kinesthetic partner is through touch. In fact, touch is the key to success in your relationship if your partner is kinesthetic. Simply telling or showing your partner the love you have for them may go almost unnoticed, but you'll be surprised at just how much a simple kiss on the cheek or a quick hug can mean. You'll also find it difficult to find a kinesthetic person who doesn't love a massage.

Expressing your love through touch can be as simple or as involved as you want it to be. The important thing is that there is touch in your relationship. The importance of touch may be difficult to understand if you are not kinesthetic, but to someone who is, touch equals love. The reverse also applies—failing to touch your kinesthetic partner may leave them feeling unloved, and their response will be slowly to withdraw from you.

Speak your partner's language

We all have a natural tendency to communicate in our preferred language—the language that we experience the world through. This can be frustrating for both people in a relationship for a number of reasons. Each person may feel they are doing everything possible to love their partner and to let them know how much they are loved, but become disheartened at the response they receive. This might be misconstrued and taken to mean that your partner doesn't love you, when in fact they do, but a. haven't understood the full impact of your actions or words and b. don't respond in the language that you best understand.

Speaking to your partner in a language other than their own is as ineffective and frustrating as speaking Italian to someone who doesn't understand that language. So don't show your love and affection in the way that you like to receive it, but in the way that will mean the most to your partner.

Learn how to really communicate with your partner. Make sure you know as much about your partner as possible. Determining the best way to show your partner just how special they are to you is simple—ask them how they like to be loved; where they like to be touched; what makes them feel special; and how you can show that you care—and then follow through on what they say. It's important to take particular note of the feedback they give you—if this means writing yourself a note then do it.

Understanding and learning your partner's language is the key to developing and maintaining a special relationship. You'll be surprised at how rewarding your relationship will become by adjusting the way you communicate with your partner. Learning and using the language that your partner understands will make a huge difference to the success of your relationship.

Open communication

You've heard the saying 'Prevention is better than cure' and this certainly applies to relationships. All too often when we realise that things aren't good, the realisation has come too late. The work required to repair a broken relationship is much more demanding than the effort required to maintain a successful relationship.

Being proactive in your relationship can save you a lot of heartache and can be extremely rewarding. Why wait until problems appear in your relationship before you do anything about them? Learn the skills you need to make your relationship work, and watch it grow.

A good way to keep your relationship on track is to practise open, honest communication. Sit down with your partner on a regular basis and really talk about your relationship. Determine how you really feel and remember to be honest. You might start by asking your partner 'Are you happy with where our relationship is heading?' 'How could I do more to add to the relationship?' 'Is there anything that I do that annoys you?' It's important to let your partner answer your questions without butting in and to remain detached—don't take offence.

at their answers. Use the feedback from your partner as a way of practising your listening skills.

It's just as important to discuss openly the good points about your relationship. Tell your partner how special they are to you. Tell them what you love about them, and why. Be specific. You might also practise praising your partner—point out their positive aspects. They may have taken the rubbish out, or cleaned up after the children, or cooked you a great meal. The more you praise their efforts, the more likely they are to repeat the action. The positive feedback and reinforcement you give and receive will only strengthen your relationship. The great thing is that open communication is so much more effective once you have made the effort to understand and communicate using your partner's representational system.

You can only work at improving your relationship if you know where to focus your efforts, and open communication with your partner gives you this insight. After all, it's much better to nip a problem in the bud than to let it grow. It's a great way to detect any gripes before they develop into a full-blown conflict. And the best way to deal with conflict and hurt is to avoid it in the first place. Work at developing the positive and eliminating the negative.

The little things always count

When we first become involved in a relationship we don't question the amount of effort or time that we devote to our partner. In fact, nothing is too difficult or too much to ask. However, the problems begin when we start to relax our commitment to the relationship. This is when the warm, fuzzy feelings start to wear off. We begin to think that the same amount of effort and attention is no longer required. This couldn't be further from the truth. For a rewarding and successful relationship continual focus and attention are essential. Remember to treat each other—there's a bit of work involved, but it can be both interesting and fun. Have a look at some of the ideas that I've come up with.

* pack a picnic with all of your favourite treats and enjoy some opera in the park

* surprise your partner and call them out of the blue just to say that you love them

* take a romantic walk somewhere special to both of you

* set a romantic mood for when your partner arrives home from work—cook up a romantic dinner, complete with candles, romantic music and a good bottle of wine

* hold hands while you are walking—recapture the innocence of the time when you were dating

* cuddle lots

* make a point of paying each other genuine compliments on a regular basis

* take each other to the movies, sit in the back row with a large tub of popcorn, and steal a cuddle and kiss when no one is looking

* book a weekend away together and pamper each other

* write a love letter and put it somewhere your partner will find it during the day, maybe in their briefcase or lunchbox

* pick a flower and leave it on your partner's pillow—what a great way to end the day!

* take some special photos together, or have them taken pro- fessionally so you can look back on these times in years to come

* go exploring together—the mountains, the beach, the city at night or the local markets

* find a new restaurant where you can enjoy Sunday brunch

* learn a foreign language and expand your minds together

* sit in the car at the beach and watch a thunder storm com- ing across the horizon

* order some take-away, rent a favourite movie and camp out on the sofa together

* have a surprise party for your partner and invite their friends

* remind your partner just how special they are to you, and why

* go snorkelling and explore a new world side by side

* make a point of scheduling your babysitter at least once a month, and enjoy an evening (or day) without the kids

* lay together, holding each other, and breathe in time—the connection will be amazing

* take time out from the real world—take the phone off the hook, and create an environment free of all distractions

* ask your partner what they would like to do and make it happen

* practise loving your partner in their particular love language

* never take your partner for granted—'thank you' are truly magic words

* open your ears when your partner is speaking—really listen to what they have to say

* rediscover each other's bodies—those magic buttons haven't disappeared!

* stay in bed all weekend!

Quality time

Did you know that you have the ability to think at around 500 words per minute, yet when it comes to verbalising your thoughts, or speaking, you can only utter around 130 words per minute? Because your mind works faster than your mouth, it's easy to find yourself focusing on something in your own mind rather than on what your partner is saying. Listening is not a skill that we are born with. To be a good listener you really have to work at it. Developing your listening skills is the key to developing the ultimate relationship with your partner.

With things today moving faster than they ever have before, being 'too busy' is a common state for many people. The pressure of work and social and family demands soon add up, and we are left with little or no time to communicate with our partner. The sad thing is that many people don't realise this until it's too late. They suddenly become aware of the lack of time spent with their partner. They feel out of touch, unaware of what is happening in their partner's life. Regaining an awareness of the relationship means spending quality time together.

Quality time doesn't include talking to your partner while thinking about what you'll do tomorrow, or listening to your partner while watching TV over their shoulder. Quality time is all about giving your undivided attention to your partner—this means that your whole attention is focused on them.

Spending quality time with your partner can be as simple as sitting on the lounge together and cuddling, or it can mean packing a picnic together and having a really good chat. It's all about giving 100 per cent of yourself to your partner at that moment in time. The key here is that the two of you are together, enjoying each other's company, making each other feel special. Spending quality time together is a great way to express the love you feel for each other.

If you can add a few suggestions to the list I've come up with then go ahead, and incorporate them into the quality time that you spend with your partner. If spending quality time together isn't one of your habits, then I suggest you make it one, and see the difference is makes.

Unconditional love

When you first become involved with someone you'll try your hardest to impress them. You'll do all that it takes. In fact, you'll do things that you wouldn't normally do, you'll wear things that you wouldn't normally wear, and you'll go places you wouldn't normally go—I'm sure you get the picture. At this stage in the relationship, your partner can do no wrong. You focus only on their positive points and the things you love about them.

As time passes and the relationship progresses, your level of commitment deepens. However, for many people, their commitment seems to be replaced by complacency. At this stage, we are no longer prepared to make the same effort; we become lazy and relax our approach. This is when our partner's bad points become clear—reality sets in and we see our partner for who they are. Although the goods points are still there, they are blurred a little by the bad.

If this focusing on the bad points is left unchecked, resentment towards your partner and your relationship will begin to set in. This of course can be the undoing of your relationship. Many people are too preoccupied with other things in their life, like work and the children, and let their relationship deteriorate without realising that it needs attention.

A relationship should be fun and exciting, regardless of the length of time you have spent together. Expand your mind and create the 'youthfulness' of your relationship once again. A relationship without any fun is set on a course of destruction. Boredom leads to frustration, and frustration causes us to look elsewhere for satisfaction. If someone else can offer you the fun and excitement that your relationship is lacking, attraction to them only increases.

A relationship is not a business transaction, so don't keep score of who did what and when. It is about unconditional love—giving and receiving without conditions placed on your love. Unconsciously, many people operate on the basis of 'I'll do this for you if you do this for me'. You might want to think of this as the 'if' theory. Over time, this kind of love builds resentment in a relationship. Taken one step further, people start to place ownership on their partner. To some, a relationship equals ownership. For the success of your relationship, concentrate on maintaining your individuality and working towards your own goals, while working with your partner towards the goals you have established together.

All too often we forget why we fell in love, and after a while we start to pick at on our partner's faults and idiosyncrasies.

Unconditional love means loving them for who and what they are. I can't emphasise enough the importance of this kind of love and acceptance. No one person will ever be all that you want them to be—a replica of yourself—and why would you want them to be? I have a favourite saying that 'If two people are exactly alike then only one of them is necessary'. It's the differences that add variety to the relationship, and variety truly is the spice of life.

Give and take from both sides is important. Developing a loving relationship is about respect and friendship. This means allowing your partner their own time and space, showing your support and encouragement, and being flexible so you can both grow together. You need to work at adding to each other's lives by doing things for one another, recognising that the need to do things for yourself is equally important.

Notes on Relationships

The Unbeatable Advantage

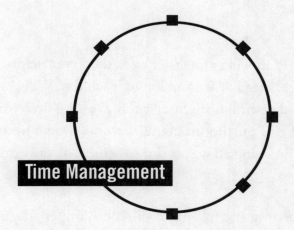

Time Management

Eliminate wasted time by making the best
use of your day, and start spending more
time on the things *you* want to do.

Time Management

With the world moving at a faster pace then ever before we all seem to be working harder and longer each day. We're starting earlier each day, finishing later each evening and working weekends. We're putting in eight, ten and twelve hour days and still not finishing all we set out to achieve at the beginning of the day.

However, burning the midnight oil is no longer the answer. We have come to realise that the number of hours we spend working is no longer proportionate to the results. We're beginning to understand that it has more to do with the quality, not the quantity, of the hours we work that is important.

So what is time management?

Time management is not about being busy, but rather about being effective, efficient and productive. It's about controlling the events in our lives and managing one of our most precious resources—time—in order to achieve specific goals.

The Pareto principle

How many times have you caught yourself saying 'I don't have enough time'? There's a different way to think about time. Instead of wishing there were more of it, accept that it is an inelastic resource, and each of us has twenty-four hours in every day—no more, no less. It's what we do with those twenty-four hours that's important—how we manage it—and that's something we have complete control over.

The Pareto principle—named after Vilfredo Pareto, a nineteenth century economist—explains why we need to set priorities in order to be effective. The rule states that eighty per cent of our time and effort produces only twenty per cent of our results, while twenty per cent of our time and effort accounts for eighty per cent of our results. So what does this mean? Simply that you can be eighty per cent effective by completing only twenty per cent of your goals, and that's not a bad return.

The idea behind the Pareto principle is to focus on the most important things first. For example, if you have a list of ten things to get done in a day, generally you will be eighty per cent effective by only completing the two most important items on your list.

Many people spend most of their time and effort working on miscellaneous tasks that aren't important, just to keep themselves busy. The problem is that once the unimportant tasks are completed, they're left at best with twenty per cent of their time to devote to the things that really count. Put your time management skills to the test and ask yourself how many times your entire day has passed without even starting the most important thing you needed to achieve. The Pareto principle is of course bad news for the workaholics who devote every waking moment to work. The workaholics out there seem to forget that they're being paid for their results and not the number of hours they work. Working extra hours doesn't guarantee success. What it does guarantee is an unhealthy balance in other areas of life, and eventually burnout.

Ultimately, we should all be aiming to get our work done faster and better, allowing us to spend more time with our family and friends and on the things we enjoy doing. Balancing your time to include things other than work will increase your energy, allow you to stay more focused and therefore become more productive when you are working. To do this you need to get into the habit of following a system of organising and prioritising time.

Stop working harder, and start working smarter

To manage your time effectively, you've got to improve the way you deal with your day and the things you need to get done. Doing this means eliminating wasted time by making the best use of every hour. There's a big difference between being busy and being productive. Recognising this difference is the first step in becoming more effective, efficient and productive. This is what working smarter, not harder is all about.

The first step to working smarter is to get yourself a daily planner or diary with one page allocated to each day. In it, write down everything that you plan to get done for that day on the appropriate page. This page now becomes your 'daily-to-do' list. This list is just the starting point—maybe you make lists already but never get around to ticking much off—the difference is what we are going to do with the list now.

Learning your ABC's

After creating your daily-to-do list, you'll need to prioritise it according to how important each of the items is. You'll find that most of the items can be easily classified according to their importance and urgency.

The 'ABC' classification is the simple and effective way to do this. The 'A' category covers things that are 'vital' or 'must do'. The 'B' category is for those items you think are 'important' or 'should do'. The 'C' items hold some value, and include things you'd like to do but aren't important or urgent.

In deciding the importance and urgency of each of the items on your list, you need to relate them back to what you want to achieve from your day. You'll find that it's much easier to effectively manage your time with your goals in mind. The chapter on Goal Setting explains the importance of setting goals and following them. Always keep the Pareto principle in mind—by doing only the most important twenty per cent of items on your list, you're well on your way to becoming eighty per cent effective. The key then to becoming the master of your time is to decide what is most important.

Taking the time to plan and prioritise your day is essential in order to make the most of your time. Don't think of it as time spent, but rather as time invested—the time you devote to planning should be one of your highest priorities, so give it the time it deserves.

Murphy's Law

Whether you decide to plan for the next day before leaving the office or when you arrive in the morning, always allow for a little flexibility in your schedule. Why? Because Murphy's Law holds true every time: everything will take longer than you expect. If you think something will take an hour you can be almost certain it will take an hour and a quarter. As a basic rule, estimate how long you think something will take, and multiply the time you allot that task by 1.25.

You've probably also found that unexpected things tend to pop up, especially when you're on a tight schedule. Again, a little extra flexibility in your day will make all the difference. If something extra does need doing simply add it to your list and classify it as either A, B, or C. Once you've finished something on your list cross it off, look over your list once again, and then move onto the next most important item.

Having a daily-to-do list guarantees that nothing will go unnoticed and will help you take control of things. You may not get around to completing everything on your list each day, but don't despair. With the things you can't manage to complete, move them onto the next day, or to a time that is more suitable, and again classify them as A, B, or C.

It is important to review your list at the end of the day, not only to see what you've accomplished, but most importantly to ensure that each of the unfinished items are rescheduled to another time and not forgotten about.

No means NO, not maybe!

To take full control of your time you need to know when to say 'No'. In fact, knowing what not to do can be more important than knowing what to do. Knowing what to say no to should be directly related to your goals—this means that you won't spend the majority of the day attending to tasks that don't really count towards anything you consider important.

There will be certain things that won't deserve your attention, and the tasks that don't help move you towards achieving your major goals should be classed as 'D' items. All 'D' items should be dumped or delegated. A good test is to ask yourself 'What is the worst possible thing that could happen if I don't complete this item? ' Your answer will determine how much, if any, time you devote to it.

Trying to stretch yourself by doing everything that is on your list means that you'll have very little, if any, time to attend to the things that really matter. Remember if the task isn't helping you achieve your goals then don't waste time doing it.

Not having enough time is no longer a valid excuse for poor time management—by planning and prioritising your activities, you will become more effective, efficient and productive in managing your time. If you've found that you were 'too busy' in the past it's probably because you didn't take the time to plan, so don't allow yourself the excuse of being 'too busy' to plan any longer!

Time management tips

Here are some helpful tips that may save you some time:

* Carry your daily planner with you everywhere—it's an invaluable item, containing all the contact names and numbers and other information you'll need throughout your day.

* Never be caught without a book and a notepad and pen when sitting on a bus or train. You can plan your day, study or prepare for the meeting you're heading to—you'll be able to make use of approximately eight hours per week that you never thought you had.

* Browse through the television guide at the beginning of the week and decide which programmes you want to watch, circle them, and only watch those you've circled.

* Schedule vacation time for yourself at the beginning of the year and write it in your daily planner otherwise it just won't happen.

* Frequently ask yourself 'What is the best use of my time right now?'

* Always date your paperwork—you'll save a lot of time when having to refer to it in the future.

* Clean up before you go home or to bed each night—this sets the next day up nicely.

* Make the most of small amounts of time by making follow-up calls or by making necessary changes to your daily planner.

* Schedule the most important items on your to-do list for first thing in the morning, or when you feel at your most alert. Make an appointment with yourself—set aside some uninterrupted time at the beginning of the day to work on your two most important tasks—you'll get twice as much done, in half the time, with half the effort.

* When someone gives you their name and contact-number, write it straight into your daily planner—that way it's there for future reference and saves you having to search for it later.

* Order a few meals at once from your favourite restaurant and freeze them—this will save you cooking time and also means you won't have to pick up the meals individually.

* Always give yourself more time than you think you'll need. Remember Murphy's Law—estimate how long you think

something will take and multiply it by 1.25. That way you'll have enough time to complete the task and won't constantly be playing catch up.

* Check your handbag or briefcase before heading out the door to make sure you've got everything you need.

* Avoid writing notes on small pieces of paper—they're difficult to work with and you're guaranteed to lose them. Instead, write everything straight into your daily planner.

* Organise your space, whether it be the office, the kitchen or your workbench, according to how often you use particular items. For example, the most frequently used things should be within reaching distance, while items you use less often can be kept a little further away.

* Keep a small tape recorder with you to record any great ideas or simply things that need doing.

Notes on Time Management

Financial Management

Start building your financial future
now, whatever your income.

Financial Management

I'd like you to start by working out how much money you've earned in the years that you've been working. Most people are not prepared for their answer, but what surprises them even more is how little they have to show for it. It's a harsh reality, I know.

What I'd like to share with you in this chapter are some of the financial principles that I've used in acquiring money, holding onto that money, and making my money earn more for me.

The importance of saving

Saving is the single most important step in setting yourself up financially. It's more important than investing your money for the simple reason that if you can't manage to save anything you'll have nothing to invest.

For most of us, saving has always been something we'll start doing tomorrow. The finances always seem too tight to start now. We continually promise ourselves that we'll start putting some money aside after we've paid the electricity bill, after we've taken that holiday, after Christmas is over, after the children have left home, after... The secret to saving is to start now—don't put it off any longer. I realise that saving your money isn't quite as exciting as spending it, but the long-term rewards will outweigh the initial pain of making it a habit to save. In fact, the good news is that saving can be simple and a lot less painful than you think.

Pay yourself first

The answer to saving is to pay yourself first. Before paying for any of your other expenses, pay yourself ten per cent of whatever you earn. The other ninety per cent of your income can be used to live on. The kind of job you have and the amount you earn is irrelevant—what matters is that you get into a habit of putting away ten per cent of your pay on a regular basis. You have to start somewhere, so start building your financial future by making the most of the job you have now and the money you're earning from it.

Paying yourself the first ten per cent of your wage may in itself sound simple—the difficult part is keeping your hands off it. You will have to avoid the temptation to spend what you've been disciplined enough to save. This can be harder than you think, but hold out and avoid the temptation and you'll find that after a short time you won't notice that you're living off less money than before. In fact, you'll manage the same as if you were living off 100 per cent of your pay.

If you don't think you are disciplined enough to save on a regular basis, it's a good idea to arrange for ten per cent of your pay to be taken out each time before you see it. Also make sure that you don't have easy access to your money, allowing you to spend it without thinking and regretting it afterwards. Quite simply, if it's not easy for you to get your hands on, you are less likely to spend it.

Saving ten per cent of your pay will add up slowly, and it won't set you up financially overnight, but the satisfaction of seeing your money building up should be enough to motivate you to keep saving on a regular basis. Saving regularly will eventually allow you to buy something substantial, while spending the ten per cent as you are now will only give you more of the same—instant gratification with no long-term gain.

Budget your expenses

I have friends who earn four times the amount that I do and others who earn half as much, yet they all have the same problem—regardless of their income, they all have too much month left at the end of their money. Basically, the more they earn, the more they spend. Isn't it interesting that the amount they spend on 'necessary expenses' just seems to increase in keeping with what they earn.

It seems that most people today have become accustomed to living beyond their means—what they want always seems to extend beyond what they can afford. Most people tend to confuse the concept of 'necessity' with 'luxury' and fail to accept that there are things that are simply beyond their financial limitations given their present financial situation—recognising this is indeed an important concept in controlling your expenditure.

Controlling your day-to-day expenses

Controlling your day-to-day expenses is extremely important in building your financial future, and the best way to do this is to develop a budget, of course remembering not to touch the ten per cent of your pay you've reserved for savings.

Budgeting allows you to direct your income appropriately—firstly, on the necessary expenses, and money permitting, towards your other 'necessities'. Budgeting will show you where you're spending your money, where you can afford to cut back, and where you can start saving even more. Quite simply, if you don't learn to budget, then you'll have a very slim chance of reaching any of your financial goals. The dream of an extended overseas holiday every year or of paying off your mortgage early can easily slip through your hands if you don't learn to take control of your finances.

You'll find it much easier and much more rewarding to budget if you have something to aim for, so set yourself a goal or an objective of how you want your money to work for you. To help you reach your financial goals, take the time to fill in the budget planner at the end of this section—you'll be surprised at the results. Now all you have to do is stick to your budget, review it every few months or so, include some flexibility and never forget that life is to be lived. And remember the key to achieving your financial goals is to spend less than you earn. Take the time to complete the budget planner at the end of this chapter.

Increase your wealth by investing wisely

As I mentioned before, simply putting aside ten per cent of your pay on a regular basis isn't going to set you up financially in the short-term. To take you one giant step closer to becoming wealthy, invest that ten per cent wisely, making your money work for you.

To make a wise decision about the investment opportunities available to you, you need to be clear about your financial goals, and also take the time to understand the types of investments and the level of risk associated with each opportunity. You don't need to know the most detailed workings of investment, but the more you know the more you'll be in control of your financial future. If you do need more advice, take the time to find a good Financial Advisor—their advice can be worth its weight in gold. Quite simply, taking lousy investment advice can see all you've worked hard for over the years simply disappear.

Once you start making a return from your investments, the key to becoming wealthy is to reinvest your returns to take advantage of compounded growth. This is where your money will really start working for you. You'll find yourself reaching your financial goals much faster the more willing you are to reinvest and not spend the returns from your investments.

When looking at the different ways you can invest and reinvest your money, please don't be tempted by the 'get rich quick' schemes and their promises. Understand that when it comes to investing 'risk equals return'. Taking risks with your money may seem tempting given the high rates of promised return, but again, high returns go hand in hand with high risks.

It isn't necessary to avoid risk altogether, but you do need to be aware of the level of risk you're taking with your investments. You'll need to find a balance between the amount of risk you can afford to take and your desire for a guaranteed return. We all realise that the higher the risk we take, the higher the return we can expect, and the greater loss if things go wrong. The opposite is also true—you can't expect outstanding returns by putting your money in a totally secure investment offering a slow, guaranteed return, like a bank account.

The amount of risk that you can afford to take will depend on your age, your financial goals and your financial situation. Obviously, the younger you are the more time you have to set yourself up financially, so the issue of risk will be less important than if you were near retirement. Also make sure you can get to your money if you need to and that the return is fair.

If a situation seems to good to be true, it probably is.

Aim to own your own home

There has been a lot said about the advantages and disadvantages of renting as opposed to owning your own home, and although renting may seem much more financially attractive in the short-term, you'll find that in the long-term owning your own home is the best way to go. In fact, I believe that owning your own home is one of the wisest investments you'll ever make. The idea of owning your own home and paying off your mortgage as quickly as possible is an essential step in setting yourself up financially.

In the short-term, renting seems to be a better option than owning your own home for a number of reasons. You'll probably find that not only will your mortgage payments be higher than the rent you were paying, but the additional costs of buying a home are quite steep at the beginning. Not only are you up for the initial expenses that include legal fees and stamp duty on your purchase, but you also have the ongoing expenses of maintenance, council rates, land taxes and the like.

What you should consider, however, is that in the long-term, paying rent is nothing but wasted money. Every cent you pay out in rent goes to pay off someone else's mortgage, namely your landlord's. Sure, in the short-term people renting tend to have more disposable income to spend on everyday living, but when you look at the long-term situation, home ownership wins hands down. Let's face it, if you have to pay for a place to live why not make your money work for you and not your landlord?

Take the time to look at the options available that allow you to deposit your wage and any other spare cash directly into your mortgage account. The repayment on a mortgage is calculated daily, therefore any amount above your minimum repayment will dramatically reduce the life of your loan. It is a great idea to also develop a good relationship with your bank manager or financial advisor, or find someone who has been successful in wealth creation, and model their successes.

Owning your own home has a number of other non-financial advantages. Unlike other areas of investment, owning a home is tangible—you experience every day the rewards that are yours as a result of disciplined saving and a commitment to seeing your goals materialise. With home ownership also comes a sense of pride—to have a home that you can call your own increases your confidence and the belief that you can achieve other goals you've set for yourself.

Protect what you have and plan for the future

Knowing how to protect your money is as important as knowing how to acquire it in the first place. Protecting the assets you've built up over the years is essential in ensuring a future income for yourself and your family. It seems strange that we work so hard for so many years to get ahead financially, yet fail to make sure that we are protected against losing the lot. Sure, we understand the importance of insuring the car, the house and the contents, but all too often we under-estimate their value. Believe me, under-valuation can cause you financial ruin.

Do your current insurance policies offer you the protection you really need? If you find that you're under-insured, make sure that you update your policies immediately, and don't be tempted to save a few dollars by under-valuing your assets. If you're not sure what your assets are worth, have a professional value them for you.

Your most important asset—yourself

Insuring your material assets is one thing, but what about insuring the all-important asset that makes it all possible—yourself! Planning for the future not only means making wise financial and investment decisions, but also planning for a time when you may no longer be able to work because of old age, sickness, disability or death. Recognising that we're not going to be around forever is an important consideration in setting up our financial future.

There are a number of insurance options available to you, including income protection, life insurance, and so on. Income protection covers your income, or part of it, in the event you can't work because of sickness or injury. The costs of income protection offered by different companies will vary widely depending upon your age, your income, your job and your health, and also on the amount and extent of cover you're looking for. The cost of income protection insurance is tax deductible, so there's no reason why you shouldn't seriously consider protecting yourself by taking out a policy.

Life insurance covers you against your untimely death. Should this happen, your family or others you nominate will receive a lump sum payout. In the event of your death you're not going to leave someone else in financial difficulty. Although we don't like to think about death, life insurance is essential if you have any family, dependent relatives or debts.

Income protection and life insurance are only two examples of the cover available to you. There are a number of other insurance options and each requires careful consideration, so take the time to get some professional advice.

Insurance is an extremely important key to wealth creation and maintenance. It's important that you have the right type and level of insurance—being under-insured can cause you financial ruin, while being over-insured is a waste of money. Remember, there's no point working hard for years on end only to risk losing it all by being inadequately protected. Insurance is a necessity, not a luxury.

Superannuation and retirement

Superannuation can seem a little confusing, but a simple way of understanding the principles behind it is to look at superannuation as a form of compulsory saving. You see, most of us would choose to spend our money rather than save it for the future and plan for the long-term. That's why superannuation is so important. It's basically a way to plan for our retirement.

Ideally, superannuation will be a long-term investment, and will be built up over the years that you are working. It's now compulsory for your employer to make contributions, and the more you can top up your superannuation fund the better. Any contributions you make are taxed lightly—that is the great advantage of adding to the contributions made by your employer.

The earlier in life you start making your own superannuation contributions the better. Starting earlier means that you can make smaller payments. Starting later in life means that the payments you make will have to be much larger to provide for a decent lifestyle when you're no longer working. It's not advisable to rely solely on the pension provided by the government for a comfortable lifestyle in your retirement—after all, there's no guarantee that the pension will be available when your time comes to retire. Think of superannuation as a wise investment, and one that will help build and maintain your financial wealth. Again, when it comes to superannuation it's best to get advice from those in the know.

Increase your ability to earn

Congratulations! You've just spent more time thinking about your financial future by reading these few pages than many people do in their entire lives. It's easy to be distracted from finding the time to think your financial situation through—it never seems to be a high priority. Most people are too busy with their day-to-day lives to really stop and consider how they could improve their situation.

Now, following the steps I've recommended will get you much closer to achieving your financial goals than you ever thought possible, but the real secret is this—realise that there are no real obstacles to stop you achieving your goals. Of course, the only obstacles that do exist are those you impose on yourself— you can continue to blame your age, your education, your skills or your background for where you are now, but they're nothing more than excuses, and excuses will continue to serve you more of the same. If you find yourself using these sorts of excuses to explain why you haven't achieved (or won't achieve in the future) an outstanding level of financial security, then refer to the section on Self-limiting Beliefs and how to eliminate them (see 'What is a belief?' on page 16).

To reach your true potential, aim to stand out from others around you by asking for what you really want from life. Don't be content with what you've achieved so far. The secret is simple—be specific. Write down exactly the life you want and the time frame in which you want to receive it. Being specific is essential—if you don't know what you want, then how do you know when you've achieved it? Please don't doubt the effectiveness of something that seems so basic. In fact, the same principles apply to any goal you'd like to achieve.

Start by asking yourself how much you'd like to earn in a year. Now, realise that life will give you what you ask for, so please don't ask for the minimum. Be daring and ask for more than you think is 'polite'—ask for an amount that is both bold and ambitious. The amount you decide on is a good indication of what you think you are worth. Your attitude toward yourself will have a much bigger impact on how successful you are financially than any other factor. If you don't believe that you can become wealthy than there is little chance that you will.

I'm sure that like most people you decided on an amount that wasn't very substantial. You have to break through any self-limiting beliefs and aim high. Why? Because life is ready to give you what you ask for. If you really want to change your life then you must change the way you think about yourself because your self-image will control your destiny. In achieving wealth it's important to work at creating a strong, positive self-image.

I can guarantee that any self-made millionaire didn't have self-limiting beliefs about their ability and worth. Their secret was to aim high, be specific in what they asked for, and believe that they could become wealthy. And don't think that they had it easy—in most cases they had to deal with huge obstacles, and this only made them more determined to succeed. Most people fail to realise how easy wealth is to acquire. They believe that they don't have the ability, or opportunity, or skills or education that other successful people have.

Look at yourself in a different light—recognise the intangible assets that you haven't made use of yet. Ask yourself what things you do well, what things you know about, and what makes you different from everyone else. This will show you what you're capable of and what you're worth. These are your personal strengths and they can be put to work to increase your wealth.

Remember this—knowledge is power, and it is the one thing that can't be taken from you. Once you know how to make and hold onto money, you can do it time and time again. Believe in yourself, respect yourself, and recognise your ability to learn.

Enjoy your work

It has been said that the true genius of life is to love what you do for a living. Would you stay in your current job if you became extremely wealthy overnight? If the answer is no then you'll have to consider changing jobs if you ever hope to achieve financial wealth. The key is to find a job that allows you to think positively about work. The goal is for your job to become as enjoyable as a hobby.

There are not many people who have become wealthy by doing something that they didn't get a real buzz from. I'm sure there will always be one or two exceptions, but most self-made millionaires are excited by the work they do. Work for them is a challenge, it is stimulating and provides an opportunity to expand their mind on a daily basis. Work should be more than simply a way to pay for the groceries or the mortgage repayments.

Consider what you can learn from your job. What are the opportunities that you haven't noticed, or that you've been taking for granted? Opening yourself up to discovery and exploration will bring a whole new meaning to your life. In fact, one of the most rewarding ways to improve your financial situation is through learning. Realise that knowledge is power when it is applied properly, and is an asset that you will have for life. Never stop learning and looking for opportunities. Being good or even great at what you do now is fine, but why stop there? To stop learning and expanding your mind is to limit your financial potential.

Enjoy your wealth

How many people do you know that seem to have more money than they know what to do with yet are still unhappy? It's too easy to get caught up in thinking that money is the most important issue in life. I know that money makes it possible to do the things you want in life with the people you love, but many people fail to realise that money is only a means to an end, and not the end itself.

Of course happiness and financial prosperity can go hand in hand, as long as you keep everything in perspective. Don't become like someone I once knew who let his money work against him. He had become so wealthy that he was constantly worried about losing the lot, and because of this his health suffered, as did his relationships. He couldn't even enjoy the simple things that his money had bought. Don't let money become an obsession. Don't make the mistake of missing out on the great things in your life now by falling into the 'If only I had more money my life would be great' trap. Achieving financial prosperity at the expense of the other areas of your life is an expensive lesson to learn. Keep in mind that life without happiness is very, very empty.

Budget Planner

MONTHLY

Category	Weekly	Annual
Home Expenses	$	
Mortgage/rent	600	31 200
Water rates	12	
Council rates	/	
House insurance	COVERED BY WK RENT.	
Contents insurance	12	
Gas	10	
Electricity	20	
Telephone	12	
Maintenance and repairs	O	
Rentals and hire purchase TV	25	
House contents: furniture, appliances, etc	10	
Other D D'S AT HOME	125	
Food		
Supermarket: milk, bread, etc	200	
Greengrocer	/	
Meat	/	
Eating out	25	
Alcohol	25	
Cigarettes	/	
Other	5	
Vehicle Expenses		
Lease/loan payments	102	
Registration	4	
Insurance: comprehensive, compulsory	8	
Petrol	30	
Repairs and maintenance	5	
Other	5	

MORTGAGE   223

Budget Planner

Category	Weekly	Annual
Family Expenses		
School fees	230	
School uniforms and books	25	
Sports and hobbies	30	
Other school expenses: excursions, etc	10	
Childcare/babysitting	/	
Clothes	40	
Gifts: Christmas, birthdays, etc	92	
Personal care	/	
Hairdresser	10	
Holidays	180	4000 (£1666)
Entertainment	20	
Newsagent: magazines and subscriptions	/	
Pets	/	
Public transport	10	
Other	5	
Health		
Medical insurance	50	
Dental	25	
Medical bills	/	
Medicines/chemist	5	
Other	5	
Income		
Household income after tax	1770	84760
Interest and dividends		
Other income	5	
Total Income	1775	
Less total expenses	1772	
Savings / MORTGAGE ON LAND	3	

Notes on Financial Management

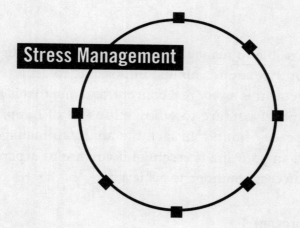

Stress Management

Live for the moment—*you* can decide
how to react to life's challenges.

Stress Management

Is it really possible to manage the level of stress in your life? It's a concept that sounds almost impossible to achieve, but stress management is a very real concept, and one that is absolutely essential if you are to enjoy a life full of happiness, health and peace of mind. In fact, the ability to manage the level of stress in your life is essential if you are to experience the kind of success you hope to achieve.

Live for the present

If you want to eliminate a huge chunk of worry in your life the first step is to live for now, in the present. Don't be concerned with the past or the future. Don't wait for some magical cure to come along that will improve your life. Live for the moment—not for yesterday or for tomorrow, but for now. Worrying about what hasn't yet happened or about what happened yesterday or last week is not only a huge waste of time, but also a guaranteed way to ensure that your stress level hits an all time high. You need to stop and smell the roses once in a while, and appreciate where you are in life today. After all, you are directly responsible for the life you are leading now.

To get a perspective on the way you handle stress, ask yourself these questions :

* Do I put off enjoying the present by worrying about the future?

* Do I let the past have a negative impact on the present by regretting something that has already happened?

How motivated am I to make the most of my life NOW?

Let's put it all into perspective

It isn't really difficult to find something to worry about, is it? We've all watched our family and friends worry, and in turn have learnt that stress and worry are a part of everyday life. If we worried only about the problems that actually exist now then we could reduce our level of stress dramatically.

Here are some figures I'm sure you'll find interesting:

* 40% of stress is caused by worrying about things that never eventuate

* 30% is spent worrying about things in the past that can't be changed

* 12% is spent worrying about health problems, either real or imaginary

* 10% is spent worrying about small, unimportant things

* 4% is spent worrying about things that you have no control over, no matter how hard you try.

That leaves just four per cent of the things you worry over that you can actually do anything about. In other words, ninety-six per cent of the things that you become stressed and anxious about are beyond your control. Do these figures put a new perspective on your life and the problems in it?

Simply by making an effort not to worry about the things you have no control over (four per cent), or the small, unimportant things in life (ten per cent) then you will be on your way to reducing your stress by almost fifteen per cent. Realise that some things are just as they are, and no amount of worry can change them. And remember that the big things in life are made up of lots of small things, just waiting to worry and stress you if you let them.

The importance of stress management—it could mean your life!

Our lives have become more hectic than ever before. With the increased pressures of work and day-to-day living it's no wonder that most of us aren't coping as well as we should be. These increasing pressures don't just test our time management skills, but can also have an adverse affect on our health.

The immune system acts as a cleansing system for your body, and the ability of your immune system to operate properly is affected directly by your level of stress. When you become stressed and worn out, your immune system becomes weakened and is unable to function properly—this increases your risk of sickness and disease. When you are stressed your body releases chemicals that directly attack your immune system, leaving you ripe for the picking. Quite simply, being stressed on a regular basis can bring about your early death. However, you can do something about it, simply by controlling how you react to situations and what you focus on.

It's all a matter of focus

As I have mentioned, what you focus on has a direct impact on how you feel and how you act. The same is true with stress. Your focus will determine both how and what you think and the outcome of your actions. You'll find that a particular situation itself isn't stressful—it's the way you react that determines your level of stress. A situation is given—the external events in any situation rarely change. This means that stress is contained in your response to the things that happen to you. You can decide whether you'll react in a stressful or a non-stressful way—it's your choice. I saw a great example of this in the actions of two women I saw at the local supermarket not too long ago.

One woman was waiting at the checkout and there were another five people in front of her, all with their trolleys loaded to the top. This woman was becoming decidedly more stressed each minute that she had to wait. She was constantly looking at her watch, checking if any of the other queues would be faster, and urging the staff-member to hurry up by uttering a few choice comments under her breath. She became so impatient that in the end she decided to leave her trolley full of food and walk out of the supermarket in a huff. Now, in the next queue, another woman was also faced with a long wait, but waiting in line wasn't an issue for her—she decided to pick up a magazine from the impulse stand and browse through it. She waited patiently in line, enjoying the chance to read the magazine without having to pay for it.

So what was the difference? Certainly not the time that each woman had to wait in line. The difference was what each woman was focusing on. The situation was the same, but the response to it was not. And it was the way that the first woman responded to the situation that caused her stress, not the situation itself. We have to take full responsibility for our lives and recognise that we each have the ability to determine the levels of stress we choose to live with on a daily basis.

When something is causing you to worry, ask yourself what you are focusing on. Train your mind to look for the best in each situation. After a while, you'll find that your mind will automatically focus on what is empowering.

The good news about stress—you can 'unlearn' it

You learnt how to become anxious and stressed by watching your parents and others that were influential during your childhood, and by modelling their responses to certain situations. Well, you can learn just as easily how to control the level of stress in your life by taking control of the situation that is causing the stress.

The first step is to realise that your problems are not usually as bad as they seem. We tend to jump to conclusions, expecting the worst in all situations. Sure, we need to be able to handle whatever may happen, but we're not too good at arming ourselves with the information we need to make the right decisions. You need to look at a problem as it really is—look at all the facts, and then reassess the problem with this new information and insight. By taking a step back, you can make the best decision to tackle any situation.

If you don't have all the information you need, your mind becomes confused and this increases your level of worry. It's impossible to make the right decisions without all the information—you're sure to fall down somewhere. You'll probably find that if you take the time to get all the information you need the problem will lose its hold on you—if it doesn't solve itself before that.

When assessing the facts it's important that you keep an open mind. It's too easy to find yourself in the position of looking for evidence just to back up how you're feeling. This doesn't give you any more of an insight into the problem—it only wastes time and effort. Make sure you're not wearing your blinkers.

Most people run around in circles trying to fix their problems. In fact, most of the time they aren't even aware of the problems they are trying to fix, yet go about attempting to fix them anyway. Trying to fix a problem without first knowing what it is, is a bit like trying to find your way through a city you've never been to before without a street directory—you'll waste a lot of effort and thought and go crazy in the process.

> To save frustration, ask yourself these four questions:
>
> What exactly is the problem? What caused the problem?
> What answers are available to me? What is the best answer?

By answering these questions you'll find that the problem will become less powerful, because the clearer you are about a situation, the more in control you are. And remember, when you feel in control, your level of stress is minimised. You can then look at the situation from a new perspective and you'll find that the problem is not as bad as it first seemed. You can then reassess the situation and prepare for the worst possible outcome by asking yourself 'Just how bad can the problem be?' Make sure that you are prepared to deal with it should it happen and decide that you can fix the problem. This will give you an even stronger sense of control.

You might feel a little uncomfortable being so up front about your problems at first, but the more directly you deal with them the better at finding stress-free solutions you'll become. Your confidence will increase, and you'll be able to deal with life as it is. Decide that you are in control of your life and how you react to each situation. Don't let the situation control you—practise the skills that give you the control to handle any situation with the minimum amount of stress and disturbance to you. Relax, and don't stress it.

You can boost your immune system and reduce your stress levels by relaxing—it may mean taking a long walk, watching a great comedy, exercising, reading the Sunday papers, or learning how to breathe properly. In fact, learning how to breathe properly is an important step in looking after your immune system. Deep breathing actually cleanses your immune system and increases the supply of oxygen, and it is oxygen that gives your cells energy. When your cells have all the oxygen they need, they are able to function properly, and you'll find that your whole body works better.

Relaxing your entire body and mind will help remove any stress and anxiety. The more relaxed you are the more effective you'll be at managing your stress. Relaxing isn't something that comes easily to everyone so it may take a little practise. The following technique should help you reach your desired state.

Take five minutes in a quiet place where you won't be disturbed and find a comfortable position to sit or lie in. Close your eyes and focus on your breathing—follow each breath in and then out, making sure to take a deep, slow breath each time. Then concentrate on relaxing every part of your body from your feet up to your head, and then back down again.

Feel each part of your body unwind. Remember a time when you felt totally relaxed—maybe it was during your favourite vacation or lying in the park on a Sunday afternoon. Remember the total experience in as much detail as possible. Allow yourself to see it, feel it, smell it, hear it and taste it. After five minutes you'll find your body is totally relaxed and probably much happier, and your mind will be focused and alert. You can then reassess the situation and tackle it from a new perspective.

Stress management tips

* Get a little sunshine. It makes you feel good, and gives your body a dose of Vitamin D, but be careful not to overdo it.

* Rest is important—it allows your body and mind a chance to recover from the working, thinking, and exercising that you put it through each day. Remember that you will need more rest the more energy you use. Take a break from it all as often as possible—aim for a three or four day break three or four times a year. Use the time to get away from work and from home.

* Make laughter and relaxation a part of your everyday life.

* Have a good stretch—you'll feel great afterwards.

* Take a drive through the countryside.

* Spend some time in a quiet place, like the library, without any distractions.

* Take a long, relaxing bath.

* Pamper yourself and enjoy a massage, pedicure or facial.

* Enjoy a glass of your favourite wine—you might even try it while taking a bath.

* Visit the art gallery or museum.

* Learn how to master the art of breathing—three deep, long breaths can do wonders.

* Watch some children playing and notice how much they make laughter a part of everything they do—there's a lesson in that for all of us.

* Cook your favourite meal with some baroque music playing in the background.

* Laugh, laugh and laugh some more—buy a joke book, and make a point of sharing the best jokes.

* Treat yourself—buy that special something that you've had your eye on.

* Make a habit of exercising—take a walk, jog, or swim—the feeling is fantastic.

* Learn to sing and/or dance, either by yourself or with a friend.

* Grab your favourite book and lie under a big old tree.

* Take yourself off to the movies.

* Walk your dog, or borrow the neighbour's.

* Go window-shopping.

* Learn to play a musical instrument.

* Sleep in on Sunday morning and enjoy a great brunch with someone special.

Notes on Stress Management

Concluding Thoughts

It has been said that success comes down to two things: knowing what you want, and knowing how to get it. The purpose of this book has been to share with you a system that helps you do exactly that. Identifying your strengths and problem areas can help you recognise what you want from life. It's then a matter of knowing how to get it, and this comes back to the concepts of attitude, skill and knowledge. The next time you find yourself wanting to improve a situation, remember to A.S.K. yourself what is holding you back.

Achieving what you want from life is a matter of taking responsibility for your thoughts and actions. It is about recognising that excelling in one or two areas of life is no real measure of success or happiness. For optimum performance, both in life and with drumming, there is a need for balance and fine-tuning. It is the difference between leading an ordinary life and one that is extraordinary, and the choice is entirely yours.

Working with some of the country's leading corporations and athletes, I have seen what a remarkable difference these concepts have made to their performance. And you have the same opportunity to realise your potential by applying these techniques to your life each day. This book is designed to be a real 'workbook'. Something that you can make notes in, and refer back to time and time again. In marketing, the golden rule is to test and measure. Without this, the marketer has no idea of where to direct efforts and resources. It's the same with life. Monitoring your progress along the way is crucial for you to achieve a higher level of success and happiness. There are twelve smaller drum skins at the back of the book. They have been included so you can continue to use this book as a guide, congratulating yourself on your successes and seeing what areas you still need to work on.

By making use of this book you'll be able to take charge of your life. You'll be able to see exactly where you are today and the direction your life is taking. You'll be able to identify what is holding you back from achieving what you want in each area of life. You'll also know the secrets to staying on track when things get a little rough.

We all have a life, whether we like the one we have or not. And if you do only have one chance at getting it right, then decide to take responsibility—now—for the direction of it. Using the concepts discussed in this book, you no longer have to be willing to settle for anything less than an outstanding level of happiness and success. Life should not be a matter of accepting or simply being grateful for what you have today. It should be about realising that you have the ability to be more than you ever thought possible. I sincerely hope that after having read this book you recognise your true potential. Go for what you really want, and enjoy the journey.

January

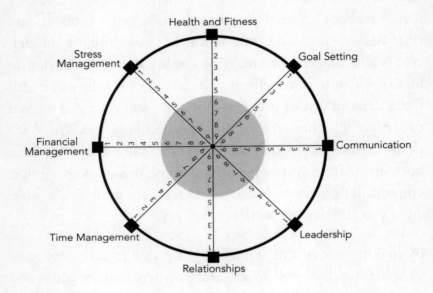

Notes

_____

_____

_____

_____

_____

_____

_____

_____

February

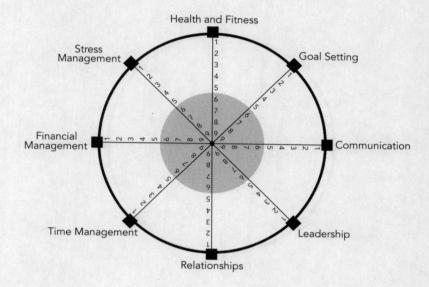

Notes
_____
_____
_____
_____
_____
_____
_____
_____
_____

March

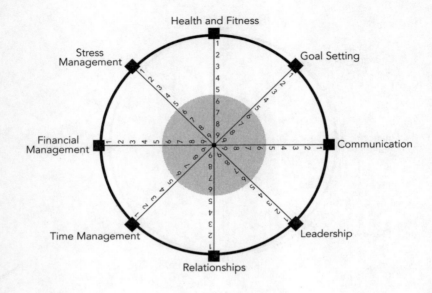

Notes

_____

_____

_____

_____

_____

_____

_____

_____

_____

April

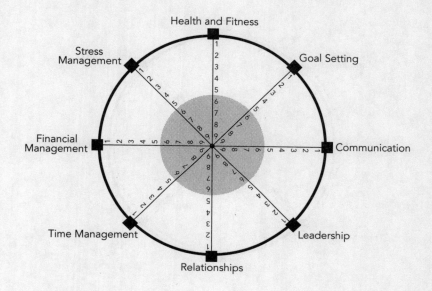

Notes

_____

_____

_____

_____

_____

_____

_____

_____

_____

May

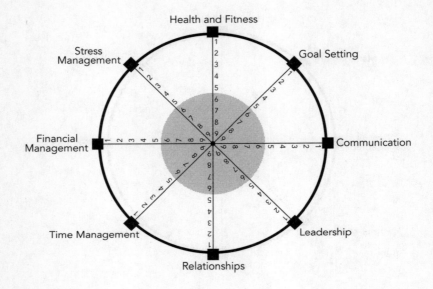

Notes

_____

_____

_____

_____

_____

_____

_____

_____

_____

June

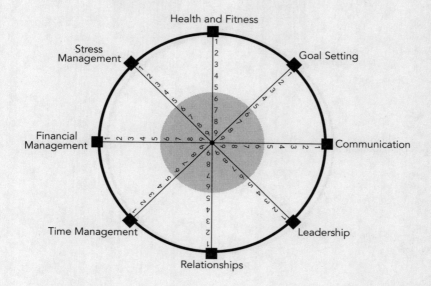

Health and Fitness

Stress Management

Goal Setting

Financial Management

Communication

Time Management

Leadership

Relationships

Notes

_____

_____

_____

_____

_____

_____

_____

_____

July

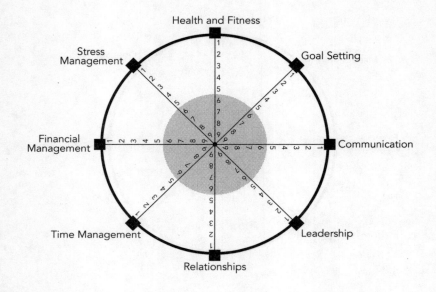

Notes
_____
_____
_____
_____
_____
_____
_____
_____
_____

August

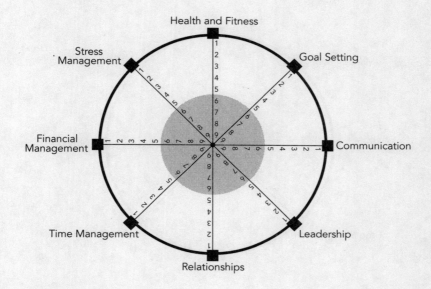

Notes

_____

_____

_____

_____

_____

_____

_____

_____

_____

September

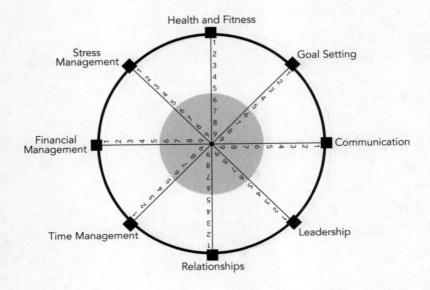

Notes
_____

_____

_____

_____

_____

_____

_____

_____

October

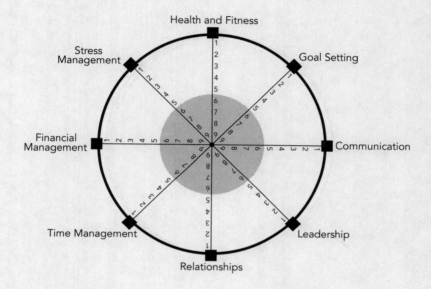

Notes

_____

_____

_____

_____

_____

_____

_____

_____

_____

November

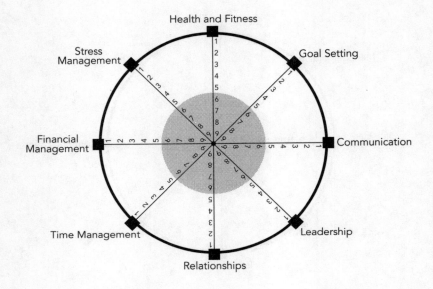

Notes

_____

_____

_____

_____

_____

_____

_____

_____

December

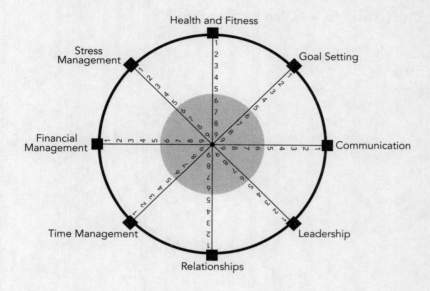

Notes

_____
_____
_____
_____
_____
_____
_____
_____
_____

I hope you have found reading *The Unbeatable Advantage* helpful and enjoyable. I'd love to hear from you about anything in the book. Please write to me at PO Box 529, Narrabeen, NSW 2101, Australia. — Glen Pattison, 1999.